AF375207

Your Free Gift!

*As a token of my thanks for taking the time to read my book, I would like to offer you a **Free Gift**:*

Leadership Lesson

from

Bhagawan Shree Rama

Subscribe to the Website

https://balvirtalwar.in

Or use the URL below to download the FREE gift.

https://balvirtalwar.in/index-php-subscribe/

Take up one idea. Make that one idea your life, dream of it, and live on it. Let the brain, the body, muscles, nerves, and every part of your body be full of that idea, and leave every other idea alone. This is the way to success and the way great spiritual giants are produced."

— *Swami Vivekananda.*

"Empower Limitless Vision" *is a captivating journey that combines ancient wisdom, spirituality, and corporate working to help you discover your inner potential and achieve lasting success in life and work.*

A newborn child radiating a divine aura inspires his parents to restart weekly group meditations. The parents respond to research queries of a young, curious gynecologist intrigued by their application of ancient knowledge to modern prenatal nurturing, aiming to unlock the child's potential as a future Corporate Guru.

The father, a guide in this transformative journey, leads his company through collective wisdom, crafting a Shared Vision and Core Values. This vision cascades into Functional Polestars, aligning each corporate function with Hindu deities. Later, he transitioned to a startup consultancy, spreading change management rooted in Vedic teachings.

"Empower Limitless Vision" is more than a book; it's a practical guide to infuse consciousness into your corporate strategy, urging you to align your dreams with timeless principles for profound self-discovery and enduring success. Embark on this extraordinary adventure and uncover the secrets to unlocking your limitless vision.

"Take the limits off of yourself. You will never rise higher than you're thinking. Create a great vision for your life."

— *Joel Osteen*

Dedication

I am immensely grateful to Almighty God. I bow to divine Maa Yati Yogeshwari Devi Ji and pay tribute to her. She has been an unending source of inspiration in all my endeavors. I acknowledge the love and blessings of my dearest parents, Sri D.V. Talwar and Late Smt Lata Rani Talwar. I am indeed grateful for the blessings of my Parents-in-Law and all elders, especially spiritual beings.

I dedicate this book to the Late Shri S.K. Jain (24 Aug. 1947 – 31 May 2015), my excellence guru, a spiritual being, and former Director (HR) of BHEL. I feel indebted to the visionary leader with missionary zeal for business excellence. His significant achievements include nurturing numerous quality and excellence initiatives and driving BHEL Haridwar to become the First PSU to win the coveted CII EXIM Bank Prize in 2006. I also thank all my seniors and colleagues for their contributions to my learning and growth throughout my 38+ year career at BHEL. I thank Shri Som Bathla for his heartfelt support in my writing, publication, and marketing journey.

This book could not have been completed without the unending support of my loving wife, Sudha. Special mention is required of Sudha, caring daughters Deepti and Divya, Son-in-Law Jatin, and little Aarav for their perpetual love and inspiration in keeping me moving. Thanks to my sister, brother, extended family, relatives, and friends for their support. Thanks to everyone, especially the readers. I seek your reviews, appreciation, suggestions, and criticism.

BALVIR TALWAR

Empower Limitless Vision

"Vision without execution is a delusion."

— Thomas A. Edison.

Contents

Empower Limitless Vision

Empower Limitless Vision

"Create a vision of who you want to be, and then live into that picture as if it were already true."

— Arnold Schwarzenegger

Introduction

"Empower Limitless Vision—Ignite Consciousness, Inspire Divinity, Align to Cosmos and Achieve Everlasting Success" is a transformative guide that awakens individuals and organizations to a profound purpose often overshadowed by the daily hustle. The book serves as a guiding light and assists individuals and corporations in delving into their personal and collective odysseys, awakening inner consciousness, nurturing divine inspiration, aligning grand dreams with the cosmos, and achieving enduring success.

Far from a mere collection of theories, the book is a manual for change, a handbook for those seeking profound success and the Truth. While individuals may continue with familiar environments, colleagues, and job roles, *"Empower Limitless Vision" guides them toward a revitalized, conscious existence, attuned to higher realms of life, drawing inspiration from the cosmos, and fulfilling life's purpose.*

The book revolutionizes thought for personal growth and emphasizes that a slight shift in the thought process can lead to a monumental change in destination. It calls readers to embrace a renewed direction and a novel approach to life that brings unparalleled happiness and a more fulfilling existence despite living the way they like. It is important to think big; as **Bill Gates said, "Microsoft was founded with a vision of a computer on every desk and in every home. We've never wavered from that vision."** Vision is limitless and executed with passion.

This book extends its universal wisdom to a broad spectrum of readers. Students and parents seeking guidance in selecting career paths for their children will find invaluable insights. Young couples aspiring for divine parenthood will discover a roadmap within these pages. Working professionals from diverse fields can visualize the greater purpose behind their work, aligning themselves with cosmic principles to achieve perpetual success. Even retirees can discover a new light, embarking on a purposeful and gratifying new chapter, as exemplified by the author's post-retirement journey.

"Empower Limitless Vision" unfolds as a roadmap, with each chapter providing a key to unlocking a different facet of holistic happiness and success. The book artfully intertwines narratives from Hindu mythology, spiritual teachings, and practical corporate insights, guiding readers toward a deeper understanding of their potential. Each stage is meticulously detailed, from igniting higher realms of consciousness to cultivating divine inspiration, aligning with cosmic principles, and achieving lasting success.

Chapters dedicated to various polestars—finance, strategy, HR, quality, marketing, engineering, technology, and supply chain management —serve as a unique bridge between mythology and modern corporate principles. Each polestar is a guiding deity and a metaphor for excellence in a specific corporate domain. Incorporating measured parameters and real-life stories associated with each polestar provides a tangible and relatable exploration.

Key Chapters and Their Significance

Igniting Higher Elms of Consciousness: Explores soulful communication, blissful group meditation, breathing techniques, and the profound concept of pure consciousness or Samadhi. Stories from spiritual leaders like Sri Ramakrishna Paramahamsa underscore the transformative power of these practices. Cultivating Divine Inspiration: Delves into collective wisdom, business excellence models, the McKinsey 7-S Model, and the importance of shared values. It guides the evolution of a shared vision, inspiring

Empower Limitless Vision

change and fostering a new beginning grounded in shared values.

Aligning Polestar to Cosmos: Embarks on a journey through different corporate domains, aligning them with corresponding deities. The finance, strategy, HR, quality, marketing, engineering, technology, and supply chain management chapters offer practical insights grounded in spiritual and corporate wisdom.

Achieving Everlasting Success: Navigates the path to self-inspiration through daily affirmations, unveiling the metrics of inspiration, and exploring the ancient secrets of perpetual success. The journey continues with reflections on blissful cultural integration and the materialization of the vision of a new world order described in the *'Sangathan Sukta'* - concluding hymns of the Rigveda.

In conclusion, "Empower Limitless Vision" invites readers to a transformative journey transcending personal and professional boundaries. The book promises a fresh perspective, enriched joy, and newfound insight regardless of age, profession, or life stage. It resonates universally, inspiring individuals from homemakers to professionals to social workers to relive in their world differently and embrace transformation. The blueprint for a fulfilling life draws inspiration from spirituality and modern corporate principles. *As the journey unfolds, readers are urged to reimagine their paths, embrace change, and guide others toward holistic and enduring success. The book is a testament to everyone's boundless potential to align with the cosmos and realize a vision that is not just corporate but cosmic—a vision that empowers limitless possibilities and endless happiness.*

-x-

About Author

Dr. Balvir Talwar, the author of the **Corporate Transformation Series**, hails from a humble, spiritually inclined middle-class family. Daily Yajna and interactions with saints instilled the essence of Vedic philosophy in him since childhood. With an excellent academic record and active participation in extracurricular activities, he graduated in mechanical engineering, followed by an MBA. As the first Ph.D. scholar in management from IIT Roorkee, he brings a unique blend of academic rigor and practical wisdom to his work.

With over 38 years of experience at a large Public Sector company, spanning roles in HR, CSR, Quality, Strategy, Corporate Communication, etc., Dr. Talwar has excelled in various pivotal roles from planner to motivational leader, catalyst, and TQ assessor. As an accomplished trainer and seeker, he has dedicated himself to promoting inclusive growth and business excellence, significantly contributing to excellence across the company. His expertise extends beyond the corporate realm, exemplified by his three-year tenure as Secretary of the UN Global Compact Network India.

His prolific contributions include numerous published papers integrating spirituality and business, reflecting his commitment to fostering holistic organizational and personal development approaches. His work has garnered recognition and over one thousand citations from academic peers. He has been a Ph.D. guide with the Open University of Mauritius. As a reviewer, he was honored with the ***Outstanding Reviewer Award*** by the Emerald Literary Network, UK, renowned for scholarly publications.

Amid the challenges of the COVID era, Dr. Talwar's leadership played a pivotal role in safeguarding the well-being of thousands of employees, contract workers, and their families during the closure and reopening of over one hundred project sites and factories.

Post-retirement, Dr. Talwar's authorial journey has been marked by a deep exploration of spirituality, leading to insightful and transformative experiences. **His books share real-life professional and spiritual learnings, aiming to inspire readers to embrace the cosmic order ('Ṛta') to bring harmony, prosperity, and bliss.**

-x-

Empower Limitless Vision

Chapter 1: Ignite Higher Elms of Consciousness

Soulful Communication

Blissful Group Meditation

Pure Consciousness and Samadhi

Vasudhaiva Kutumbakam

Soulful Communication

"Soulful communication is the art of connecting with others at the deepest level, where words become unnecessary, and hearts speak the language of understanding."

As the days passed after the birth of their blissful son, Rishi, a warm and comforting routine settled into their lives. With his bright golden aura, Rishi had brought immeasurable joy to their home. Shruti had emerged from childbirth feeling healthy and strong after a normal delivery. She cherished the moments when she could cradle Rishi in her arms, her heart brimming with maternal love.

Her husband, Aryan, an engineer from IIT Delhi and an MBA from Stanford University, had taken a three-week paternal leave. He was about to return to work at the Financial Services MNC in New York, where he had worked since 2018. Initially hired as Manager of IT, his career soared, leading to his promotion to Senior Manager of IT in 2019. Aryan lived a lavish life in Manhattan and even acquired a Ferrari on his 30th birthday in 2019. Due to the high-pressure job, he could not visit his parents in India for three years.

However, tragedy struck when his parents, both doctors, succumbed to COVID-19 while serving patients in 2021. It led to a profound change in Aryan's life. He sought solace in the Himalayas, encountering a wise Sadhu who helped him through his depression.

During this transformative period, Aryan met his soulmate, Shruti, an IT engineer, in a temple while she was on spiritual tourism. They both learned meditation and more from the wise Himalayan Sadhu, who blessed them to marry.

On his return to New York from India after six months, Aryan transformed his role and became the Chief Learning Officer, courtesy of his kind-hearted CEO, John. He organized meditation workshops for top management, colleagues, other employees, families, friends, and the public to spread eternal peace and wisdom. After a few months, as foreseen by the wise Sadhu, Aryan married Shruti on 15 January 2022. Incidentally, her company transferred Shruti to the USA for one year to lead an IT project in Chicago.

Following utmost self-restraint and learning from ancient wisdom, they planned for their child. They followed ancient rituals and Samskara in letter and spirit, coupled with guidance from the wise Himalayan Sadhu, and were blessed with a son, Rishi. The transition from full-time dad to working professional loomed in Aryan's mind, but for now, he relished these precious days of bonding with his wife and newborn divine son.

This morning, they sat beside their two-week-old son, Rishi, who slept peacefully with a gentle smile on his tiny face. Rishi's expressions flickered as if engaged in a lively dream conversation. Unnoticed, Shruti's mother observed the heartwarming scene, witnessing the love and joy emanating from Shruti and Aryan. A warm smile graced her lips as she quietly left, reassured by the love surrounding her daughter.

Time passed in blissful silence. The room was enveloped in a serene stillness. Their eyes spoke volumes, delving into shared history and contemplating an uncertain future. This wordless communion painted intricate strokes on the canvas of their connection, conveying thoughts, feelings, and desires that words could never capture. It was an intimate dance of emotions, a dialogue of souls. *Their silent conversation was a testament to the profound power of nonverbal communication, affirming that love could be spoken without uttering a single word.*

Breaking the tranquil silence, Aryan gently squeezed Shruti's hand, his eyes filled with love and curiosity. "What next?" he whispered. Shruti stirred from her reverie, her head resting on Aryan's shoulder, and met his gaze with an affectionate intensity that needed no verbal response. They understood their journey as parents had just begun, navigating the path ahead with love.

With a contented sigh, she nestled closer to Aryan, seeking solace in their shared embrace. Without speaking a word, their love and baby Rishi spoke volumes, assuring them of endless possibilities and infinite joy in the future.

Reflecting on soulful communication, Aryan observed Shruti's silent immersion in the language of love. He contemplated integrating such communication into the hectic office environment, envisioning a workplace filled with mutual love and belief. Aryan pondered creating an atmosphere where tasks are approached with unity, minimizing the need for spoken words. He pondered, "How do you create an office atmosphere filled with mutual faith, where every interaction is infused with the language of love? Can we foster an environment where big or small tasks are approached with unity and cooperation, minimizing the need for spoken words? How can we make unwritten and nonverbal expressions a central and effective mode of communication in our professional lives?"

He drew inspiration from the natural world and the animal kingdom, where communication often transcended words. In this realm, love and understanding formed the basis of interaction, and Aryan pondered whether humans could embrace a similar approach.

"Soulful communication," he mused, "requires a foundation of eternal love." Saints and highly evolved souls have been practicing this communication for ages. It was how a mother communicated with her newborn child, the way a guru imparted wisdom to devoted disciples, even across great distances. Aryan recalled the profound example of soulful communication in the Bhagavad Gita, where Lord Krishna clarified Arjuna's doubts, guiding him on the path of righteousness before the Mahabharata War. When clarity reigns supreme and doubts are dispelled, dedication and devotion reach their zenith.

*Aryan then delved into the **essence of perfect communication**, which, he believed, lay in the common answers to the six fundamental questions, often expressed as **5W1H:*** **What, Why, When, Where, Who, and How**. When all stakeholders reached a consensus on these questions and shared a

Empower Limitless Vision

uniform understanding of the task's importance, their performance soared to new heights.

This state transcended all barriers of time, bringing humankind into a realm of the fourth dimension, where each moment could be compressed or expanded at will. Through time compression, remarkable records of task performance were achieved, while the expansion of moments allowed for the enrichment of blissful states of love.

Aryan asserted that the key to unlocking these experiences resided in the art of soulful communication. This pathway might lead humanity toward the cherished ideal of **"Vasudhaiva Kutumbakam,"** *the concept that "The Whole World is One Family."* In this interconnected world, people would communicate through the language of love, fostering unity and harmony on a global scale.

With these thoughts swirling in his mind, Aryan contemplated: Is this mode of communication better or worse than conventional ways of interaction? How can the profound power of soulful workplace interaction, where love and understanding drive Cooperation, Collaboration, and Commitment, be infused?

He came out of his thoughts when Shruti asked him to get up as her mother prepared and brought the tea. Together, they enjoyed the tea with cookies while Aryan shared his newfound intuitive thoughts about workplace communication, leading to everlasting commitment, which he had received during a deep-thinking state.

Empower Limitless Vision

Shruti appreciated the concept, adding that the corporate world would take a long time to recognize its potential, and perhaps little Rishi could implement such thoughts as a "Corporate Guru." Shruti's mother remarked, "Eternal Love is the essence of soulful communication, which leads to a mother's commitment to her child." Unaware of all this conversation, little Rishi smiled and enjoyed his world.

-X-

Empower Limitless Vision

Blissful Group Meditation

"The wise, seeing the same Self in all, are not attached to the body and mind. Such realized beings remain ever calm and undisturbed."
- Bhagavad Gita.

The following day, Aryan and Shruti prepared for their first group meditation at home since Rishi's birth. Understanding the power of meditation from the Upanishads and Vedas, they believed that group meditation enhances inner peace and resilience.

Planning for any disruptions during meditation, Shruti would take Rishi inside if he cried, ensuring Aryan could continue guiding the meditation without disturbing their guests. Group meditation had become a weekly routine for the past few months in their new home in Bridgewater, New Jersey, close to the Ganesha Shiva temple, around 40 miles from Manhattan.

Initiated at the request of the "Young Thinktank," led by Sophia, a dynamic group of Aryan colleagues from various departments had turned group meditation into a weekly get-together at their home. Sophia, who worked alongside Aryan in HR, was pivotal in organizing training programs and workshops. In these events, group meditation had blossomed into a company norm. The other members of the Young Thinktank comprised Robin, a CFA working in Finance; James, an MBA in Marketing; Adam, a B.Tech in IT; Emma, an MBA in HR; and Hanna, a Ph.D. in R&D.

Due to Shruti's pregnancy and Rishi's birth, they temporarily moved the meditation sessions to a nearby temple for the past three weeks. Now, joyously resuming at home, Sophia and the group set the room's ambiance with fresh flowers. Nancy, a cherished neighbor considered

Empower Limitless Vision

family, joined them, eager to witness Rishi's inaugural participation. Soon after, special guests Mr. and Mrs. Sharma, who held Aryan and Shruti dear as their children, graced the gathering. Shruti's Gynecologist, Dr. Shweta, and her colleague, Dr. Markesic, followed them.

Dr. Shweta felt a divine connection with the couple when they met her for the first time. *She had rarely felt such warmth and connectivity with patients in her 35-year career. She* soon realized that Aryan's mother had been her classmate at AIIMS, New Delhi, and they disconnected when Dr. Shweta relocated to the USA. *Deeply moved by Aryan's parents' selfless service during the COVID era, she offered her medical services to their child as a tribute, free of charge. This selfless gesture left the couple astounded.*

Upon confirming pregnancy, Aryan and Shruti volunteered for Dr. Markesic's scientific study on Hindu rituals and the birth of a divine child. The doctor, intrigued by their practices and the accuracy of their claims, embraced the opportunity as a research project to learn about the birth of a divine child. *Both doctors, busy as they were, wholeheartedly committed to this special occasion. Dr. Markesic, a Christian, found Hinduism fascinating and discovered striking similarities in specific thoughts reflecting the convergence of beliefs.*

As the appointed time neared, neighbors and regular meditation participants gathered, intrigued by Rishi's anticipated participation, creating an expectation of a tranquil session with around 20 to 25 attendees. Aryan graciously welcomed the guests into the meditation room, dressed in a pristine white cotton kurta pajama that emanated comfort, modesty, and spiritual presence. He was cross-legged on a mat at 9:00 AM and prepared to guide the meditation. He postured upright in meditative mudra with palms resting on his lap and thumbs lightly touching index

Empower Limitless Vision

fingers, facilitating deep, unhindered breathing, balancing, and channeling energy during the session.

Simultaneously, Shruti entered the room with baby Rishi cradled in her arms. Her pastel-colored saree, adorned with delicate embroidery, exuded grace and sophistication, creating an aura of serenity. Baby Rishi, dressed in a designer baby outfit, charmed everyone with his gentle smile. Even before the meditation began, the room was filled with fresh flowers, promising a profoundly serene and spiritually enriching experience for all participants.

Abdominal Breathing

*Aryan introduced participants to stomach or abdominal breathing. He encouraged them to focus on deep breathing, emphasizing inhalation into the lower part of the lungs, the diaphragm's engagement, and the abdomen's expansion as they inhaled. This technique enhanced oxygen intake, promoted increased energy levels, and improved mental clarity. Aryan elucidated the numerous benefits of this breathing style, which included triggering the relaxation response, reducing stress and anxiety, stimulating the vagus nerve, lowering heart rate and blood pressure, detoxifying the body, and enhancing digestion. It strengthens the diaphragm and improves lung capacity, which benefits asthma patients. **He shared that a saint living in the Himalayas for over two centuries credited his robust health and longevity to practicing abdominal breathing and maintaining a straight backbone.***

After abdominal breathing, Aryan transitioned the group into Nadi Shodhana, known as Anulom Vilom or Alternate Nostril Breathing. This yogic breathing technique and a traditional Indian practice harmonize the body's energy flow by alternating the breath between the left and right nostrils. Aryan demonstrated the method, instructing participants to use their right thumb to close the right nostril and their right middle and ring fingers to close the left nostril. The process involved inhaling deeply, starting through the left nostril, exhaling through the right nostril, and then reversing the pattern to complete one cycle. Repeat the cycle continuously for some time. Aryan explained that this practice promoted a calm mind, reduced stress and anxiety, balanced brain hemispheres, purified energy channels in the body, lowered blood pressure, boosted the immune system, and improved sleep quality.

Group Meditation

With participants now attuned to their breath and relaxed, Aryan gently transitioned them into the meditation phase. He began by encouraging participants to find a comfortable posture, sitting or lying down, with their backs straight. He advised them to gently close their eyes and turn their focus inward, observing the sensation of their breath as it entered and exited their nostrils or the rise and fall of their chest and abdomen. Aryan acknowledged that the mind might wander, but he urged participants not to judge or attach to their thoughts, instead gently redirecting their attention back to their breath, anchoring them in the present moment.

Aryan asked participants to be comfortable with their natural breathing and observe the sensation of the breath as it enters and exits the nostrils or the rise and fall of their chest or abdomen. It anchors the mind to the present moment. Your mind will likely wander. When it does, gently acknowledge the thought or distraction without judgment and bring your focus back to your breath. It's normal for ideas to arise; the key is not to attach to them and to remain mindful and focused on observing the breath. That's all. It is a simple meditation, and anyone can practice it. Begin meditation with a 5-10-minute session and gradually increase the duration as you become more comfortable. Aryan explained in detail as a few new people joined the session today. Group meditation was free of cost, and everyone was welcome to attend.

Aryan emphasized that meditation is a skill that improves with practice and encouraged participants to start with short sessions, gradually extending the duration as they become more comfortable. He acknowledged that there are many ways to meditate, and the path to inner peace and reduced stress varies from individual to individual.

In various religious practices, people learn numerous ways to meditate. One approach is to do a body scan, where you systematically focus on each part of your body, releasing tension and promoting relaxation. Another method is to follow guided meditation apps or recordings. Naam Japa is yet another popular way to meditate, where one continuously recites a mantra recommended by a Guru or meditation teacher, or any mantra that fascinated him, like Aum, Om Namah Shivaya, Gayatri Mantra, Hare Rama Hare Krishna, etc. One may even practice Kriya Yoga, follow Art of Living meditation, Sahaj Marg meditation, Sahaj Yoga Meditation, Kundalini Yoga, etc. The bottom line remains that one should be aware of the present moment and experience inner bliss.

All these practices lead to a single destination - a 'Transcendental state or highest state of Spiritual Joy' from different routes and modes as per one's convenience and desire. *Initially, one may examine many methods before adoption, like searching for a suitable life partner. But once you marry, accept it as your destiny and be with your soulmate. Similarly, consistently follow your meditation technique to reach the destination. All methods' goals are the same as ever, passing through different routes. Your inner consciousness and past Karma often unconsciously direct you to follow a suitable path.*

Aryan concluded that the easiest way to attain a Transcendental State is OM or AUM meditation. Let us focus on OM meditation for a few minutes before completing the session. During this period, little Rishi kept spreading his mysterious smile in a serene environment; no one could see him with their eyes closed except his mother. Shruti was watching her son with her mental eyes and enjoying his smile.

OM – Meditation

Aryan asked for a group chant of "OM" or "AUM," a sacred cosmic sound symbolizing ultimate truth and unity. As participants chanted OM and focused on their Heart Chakra, Aryan explained the significance of this primordial sound, which connected individuals with the divine energy present in all existence. He noted that "OM" represented creation, preservation, and destruction, and its proper pronunciation and resonance held immense spiritual power.

*He explained how to pronounce the OM. "O" should be six times louder and longer than "M" – 'OOOOOOM.' In Sanskrit, "O" is a diphthong– a subtle speech sound that begins with one vowel and changes to another within the same syllable. This "O" sound starts with an "A" sound, as in "law," and ends with a "U" sound, as in "put." Combining these two vowel sounds in this diphthong produces a pure sound. **When pronouncing OM, it should sound like "home" without the beginning "h" sound. The sound should emanate from the navel with a deep and harmonious vibration and gradually rise upwards to resonate in the nostrils.***

The meditation session reached its peaceful conclusion at 9:45 AM. Aryan gently guided participants back to a state of wakefulness, instructing them to rub their

Empower Limitless Vision

hands together and place them over their eyes and faces to feel the warmth before slowly opening them. The session had been a profoundly blissful experience for everyone, facilitated by the serene presence of little Rishi, who had spent the entire time spreading his divine energy with his radiant smile.

While most guests returned after the session, a few stayed behind. Dr. Markesic took Rishi from Shruti on her lap. Nancy and Sophia went to the kitchen along with Shruti. Mr. and Mrs. Sharma, Shruti's Gynecologist, Dr. Shweta, and Dr. Markesic remained in the meditation room, interacting with Aryan while Dr. Markesic had some queries.

-X-

Pure Consciousness or Samadhi

"In the heart certainly is the Atman; the mind is its dwelling place. This one goes forth dreaming, for it is in the state of dreaming that it is set free, being united with intelligence." - Atharva Veda 12.1.1

Following the group meditation, Dr. Markesic, a young gynecologist and researcher, cradled little Rishi. She approached a picture of "OM" displayed in the room, which depicted various states of consciousness. She understood that the image alludes to going beyond ordinary states of consciousness, possibly indicating a state of heightened awareness or realization during dreaming. Intrigued and eager to comprehend further, she turned to Aryan and asked for an explanation of the picture's significance. Mr. and Mrs. Sharma and Dr. Shweta were curious and joined the conversation.

OM and Various States of Consciousness

Aryan elucidated the profound significance of "OM" as the primordial and seed mantra of the universe. He described how "OM" embodies the creative energy and divine vibration permeating the cosmos. This sacred symbol represents the universe, encapsulating the ultimate reality. Aryan emphasized that "OM" encompasses all aspects of the universe, symbolizing its eternal nature and serving as a powerful aid in meditation and prayer. He explained that "OM" is synonymous with intuition and knowledge, acting as a bridge to the Third Eye within the Chakra system.

Furthermore, Aryan elaborated that **"OM" symbolizes the harmonious union of spirit, body, and mind, reflecting the continuous cycle of Birth, Life, and Death**. Drawing from the Katha Upanishad, he

Empower Limitless Vision

explained that "OM" is vital in directing the life force upwards, awakening the Kundalini energy, and dispelling ignorance.

The picture represents the "OM" symbol and depicts the evolution of consciousness from "OM" as per the Mandukya Upanishad mantra that elucidates this concept, which states:

"The past, the present, and the future, all that was, all that will be, is OM…. All else that may exist beyond the bounds of time is OM."

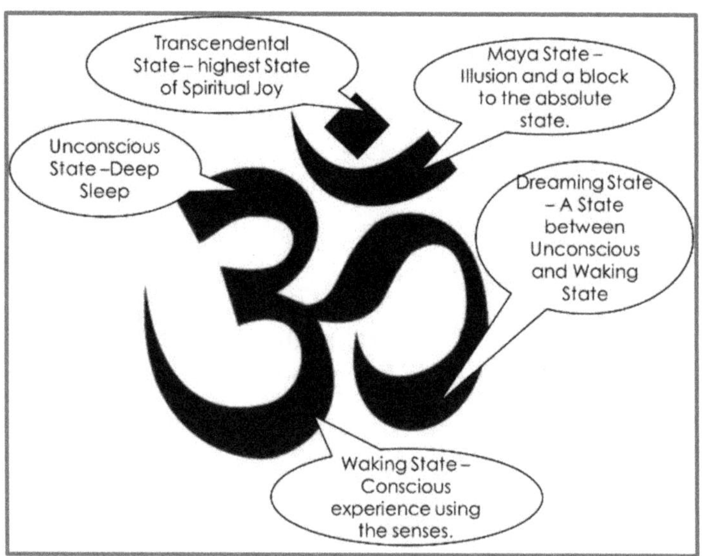

The sound of AUM in the OM Symbol corresponds to the four states of consciousness, namely:

- *"A" in AUM represents the Waking State (Jagrit) - Our conscious mind using senses or Physical State;*

- *"U" in AUM represents Dream State (Swapan) - Our subtle world or active unconscious – A state between the Unconscious and Waking State;*

- *"M" in AUM represents the Unconscious State (Deep Sleep or Death) - Our latent unconscious;*

- *Positioned above the "OM" symbol, the Moon icon symbolizes the state of illusion or Maya.* It mirrors our perceptions and reactions to the external world, encompassing our emotional responses, such as love and hatred. *Like the ever-changing phases of the Moon, as it traverses through different Nakshatras, our reactions to the world are in constant flux. They fluctuate from the New Moon Day (Amavasya) to the Full Moon Day (Purnima) and vice versa.* The Moon symbol serves as a shield, potentially drawing us back into the previous three states of consciousness (Waking, Dreaming, and Unconscious State).

- Positioned directly above the Moon symbol, the "Chandra Bindu" point *represents the fourth state of consciousness. It signifies "Silence" following the utterance of "AUM" or the Transcendental State (Turiya or Samadhi) — a state of pure consciousness and the highest manifestation of Ananda (bliss).*

During meditation, the goal is to attain profound silence, the highest form of consciousness. Silence encapsulates the essence of human existence and serves as the purpose of meditation itself. The primary aim is to achieve this blissful state of "Silence" after chanting "AUM." Silence signifies a state of thoughtlessness, an Ananda (bliss) that transcends expression through our senses. This state is scarce and can only be attained by a select few.

Often, we engage in various meditation techniques, rituals, prayers, mantras, and

Empower Limitless Vision

emotional responses. However, the true purpose of meditation is to transcend all of these. Think of meditation as the staircase leading to a temple. To seek blessings from the Deity inside the temple, one must leave the stairs behind and enter the sacred space. Yet, a few among millions can journey from the stairs to the Deity or the state of Samadhi. To illustrate this concept further, Aryan shared the enlightening story of Sri Ramakrishna Paramahamsa, Swami Vivekananda's spiritual mentor.

Sri Ramakrishna Paramahamsa Story

Sri Ramakrishna Paramahamsa was an ardent devotee of Goddess Kali, for whom Kali was not just a deity but a living reality. He would often see the Divine Mother's form, receive Her instructions, and bask in Her guidance. She danced before him, ate from his hands, responded to his calls, and left him in a state of pure ecstasy. It was not a hallucination but reality. His consciousness was so crystallized that whatever form he wished became a reality.

One day, Sri Ramakrishna was sitting on the banks of the Hoogli River when Swami Totapuri, a great and rare yogi who attained oneness with God, came that way. Recognizing Sri Ramakrishna's advanced devotion and potential for enlightenment, Swami Totapuri advised him that while he possessed the necessary energy, he needed to empower his awareness. Sri Ramakrishna agreed, and Swami Totapuri initiated him into Vedantic meditation, guiding him to transcend the Divine Mother and the ecstasy of Her presence. *With Swami Totapuri's blessings, Sri Ramakrishna achieved Samadhi, or the vision of God, in his very first attempt, remaining absorbed in this state for three consecutive days!*

It marked his transformation into a Paramahamsa, a fully enlightened being. Until then, he had been a lover,

Empower Limitless Vision

devotee, and child of the Mother Goddess he deeply cherished. ***Aryan concluded by explaining that "Silence" represented the union with God, the realization of "Aham Brahmasmi," which means "I am the Brahman," as expressed in Vedanta.***

Mrs. Sharma, a devout, wise older woman, offered her blessings to Aryan after listening attentively. She remarked, "I have seen the OM symbol many times but never knew such a profound interpretation of its meaning." *Aryan responded, "I am equally astonished. I wasn't speaking; it felt like some hidden force poured these words into my mouth about these insights."* Little Rishi, mysteriously smiling, gazed at them.

Mrs. Sharma explained, ***"When the environment is pure and filled with positive vibes, the collective consciousness and wisdom ascend to higher dimensions, revealing new facets of divinity, benefiting everyone."*** Dr. Markesic's curiosity helped everyone, inspiring and rejuvenating their quest to explore the divine.

Meanwhile, Shruti, Nancy, and Sophia prepared breakfast and called everyone to the Drawing Room to enjoy breakfast together.

-x-

Vasudhaiva Kutumbakam

If you feel pain, you are alive. If you think about other people's pain, you are human.
— Leo Tolstoy

Dr. Markesic had numerous queries about the significance of the rituals followed during pregnancy and till the birth of baby Rishi. She had seen the rituals happening physically, but was keen to know their importance and the science behind each ritual for her research. While she was engrossed in Aryan's explanation of "OM" and pure consciousness, Shruti's call to everyone to join breakfast interrupted her thoughts.

To everyone's astonishment, Dr. Markesic requested that all accompany her to Aryan's bedroom before breakfast. She wished to admire a beautiful poster of Lord Krishna as a child. The child in the poster strikingly resembled little Rishi. Curious, Dr. Markesic inquired about the secret phenomenon from Shruti. **Shruti acknowledged that she had gazed at the picture countless times during pregnancy, envisioning that her son would mirror its virtuous and identical appearance. This vision had manifested into reality.** Her Gynaecologist, Dr. Shweta, said that she had witnessed several cases where the mother's thoughts about the child during pregnancy have been manifested into reality. For her young colleague, Markesic, it was the first blissful experience.

Shruti explained further that she thought her child would be a Corporate Guru and that he would impart ancient wisdom about Indian Ethos and Culture globally. The discussion continued over a delightful breakfast. On a query about Indian Ethos during breakfast, *Aryan said that*

Empower Limitless Vision

the essence of Sanatana Dharma lies in "Vasudhaiva Kutumbakam," (वसुधैव कुटुम्बकम्) a Sanskrit phrase signifying that "the world is one family." Rooted in Indian spirituality and philosophy, it fosters global harmony, dignity, and accountability for a more inclusive and peaceful world.

Vasudhaiva Kutumbakam originates in ancient Indian scripture, the Upanishads, emphasizing universal brotherhood and the interconnectedness of all beings. This timeless concept has recently gained popularity, symbolizing India's cultural heritage and values of compassion, diversity, and global unity.

Incorporating Vasudhaiva Kutumbakam into daily life involves embracing diversity, practicing empathy, promoting kindness, leading by example, and educating others about our shared values. It contributes to a world that values diversity and fosters a sense of oneness. It emphasizes healthy relations and connectedness among people regardless of their backgrounds. It promotes peace, encourages respect for diversity, nurtures global responsibility, and supports sustainability. It contributes to a more peaceful, understanding, and sustainable world by fostering unity, respect, and global accountability. Aryan invited everyone to relook at their relationship with little Rishi based on this concept.

Shruti explained, "I am Rishi's mother, and Aryan is his father. My mother, Rishi's Nani, has a special place in his life. Dr. Shweta was a classmate of Aryan's mother. She cared for us like a mother and never charged us for her consultation fees and even the nursing home expenses, despite our repeated requests to pay at least for the actual expenses incurred by her. Rather, Dr. Shweta always blessed us, fed us delicious food, and gave us numerous gifts. She is

Aryan's mother's sister, or 'Masi,' and, in this way, she's become Doctor Dadi to Rishi. Upon hearing this, Dr. Shweta became emotional and happily embraced her newfound connection with little Rishi. This revelation piqued everyone's interest, and they wanted to know more about defining a relationship with Rishi.

Shruti continued, "Even though Aryan has lost his parents, Mr. and Mrs. Sharma have always showered their love on us, like parents. Mrs. Sharma prepared 'Panjiri,' a nutritious mixture of dry fruits, herbs, cow's ghee, and other ingredients suitable for a new mother's recovery. They are like elder siblings to Aryan's parents. So, they are our Tauji and Taiji and little Rishi's Dada and Dadi. Mr. and Mrs. Sharma smiled and blessed the family with unwavering love.

Nancy added, "I consider Shruti my elder sister, which makes me Masi to Rishi. Sophia said, "I work closely with Aryan and consider him my guide and elder brother. Therefore, I'm Bua to little Rishi."

As all eyes turned to Dr. Markesic, who appeared puzzled and surprised by these newfound relationships, she finally said, "I'm like a Doctor Aunt to little Rishi." It elicited smiles from everyone. The home atmosphere had transformed into a family gathering rather than some guests visiting a friendly family. Dr. Markesic said, "Now I truly understand the profound impact and meaning of Vasudhaiva Kutumbakam."

Mrs. Sharma said, "This is how we used to live in India, especially in small towns and villages, where we nurtured relationships based on mutual love, respect, and dignity." Everyone expressed their gratitude to Aryan and Shruti for this heartwarming morning. They departed for their homes except for Dr. Markesic and Nancy.

Dr. Markesic had lingering questions about her research project, eager to delve into the rich realm of ancient Indian Ethos and its impact on human life. Nancy, too, was keen to participate in this exciting conversation. She had come to their residence after a few days and was eager to spend some more time with her lovely family and Rishi. It was time to feed Rishi; thus, Shruti and her mother went inside to tend to him. Aryan, Dr. Markesic, and Nancy remained in the Drawing Room to continue their conversation.

Aryan began by sharing insights into Hindu mythology's "Samskara" concept, highlighting its role in controlling human temptations and purifying the mind. He explained that ***"Samskara" encompasses both external rituals and inner resolutions, with each ceremony serving spiritual, cultural, and psychological purposes, ushering individuals into the next stage of life, attaching specific duties and privileges.***

Aryan explained that half of the sixteen Samskara ceremonies are conducted during pregnancy and early childhood till the preschool stage, signifying permanent impressions in a child's mind. Dr. Shweta said a child undergoes crucial brain development during the first five years of life. Various studies in neuroscience and early childhood education indicate that this period is particularly influential for learning. The brain experiences rapid growth and is highly receptive to environmental stimuli and experiences.

Mrs. Sharma added the initial three Samskara performed before the child's birth are Garbhadan (conception), Pumsavana (a rite celebrating the fetus during the 2nd or 3rd month of pregnancy), and Simanatonayan (a ceremony to protect the unborn baby and the mother during the 7th or 8th month of pregnancy). The subsequent two rituals, Jatakarman (a rite celebrating birth) and Namakarana (naming the child), occur the first month after birth. Following these, there are additional ceremonies, including Annaprashana (the baby's first feeding of solid food after five months of age), Mundan (the baby's first haircut during 1st or 2nd year of age), and Upanayana (the entry into school rite).

Dr. Markesic and Nancy were keen to know how Shruti could confidently say their son would become a Corporate Guru and guide global businesses for ethical conduct.

Shruti emphasized the profound impact of pregnancy on a child's development, particularly during the eighth month, known as "Dohirda." She explained how a mother's thoughts and emotions during this stage significantly influence the child's mind, intellect, and spiritual growth.

She said ancient wisdom suggests that the mother can modify the Samskara (impressions) from the child's previous incarnation, shaping the child's mental and spiritual growth through her thoughts during pregnancy. For example, during Mahabharata, Abhimanyu's mother imparted knowledge on breaking Chakravyuh while pregnant. They had meticulously planned Rishi's upbringing to nurture him into a "Corporate Guru" who would guide global businesses to work ethically for the wellbeing of humankind. Nancy quipped, "That is why Shruti took a long leave."

Shruti continued and said they celebrated their first wedding anniversary blissfully with a meditation camp at a New Jersey orphanage in January 2023, followed by gestures of kindness and support, such as providing food

Empower Limitless Vision

and donations to the orphanage. They used to meditate together daily. Aryan played a crucial role in shaping his company's vision and facilitating Shruti's mother's visa and air tickets to join them in early February. *Aryan was instrumental in developing the Functional Polestar statements incorporating spirituality for his company during February and March 23. On each occasion, Aryan and Shruti discussed the details of the deliberations held to evolve the polestars. Throughout, they felt Rishi had imbibed these values while in the womb.*

Little Rishi's birth on March 28, 2023, filled the couple with wonder, as his enchanting smile and golden aura resembled the photo of Lord Krishna at their home. Dr. Markesic expressed her interest in further details for her research, to which Aryan and Shruti agreed, promising to share more insights in their next meeting.

Following their discussions, Dr. Markesic and Nancy joined the couple for lunch before heading back home, feeling content and enlightened by the extraordinary journey they had embarked upon.

-x-

Chapter 2: Cultivate Divine Inspiration

Acquire Collective Wisdom

Evolve a Shared Vision

Inspire the Change

Inculcate Shared Values

Maternal Influence on Unborn Child

Empower Limitless Vision

Empower Limitless Vision

Acquire Collective Wisdom

"To improve is to change; to be perfect is to change often."   - Winston Churchill

On Monday, April 17, 2023, Aryan rejoined his office after availing himself of paternity leave following the birth of his blissful son, Rishi, three weeks ago. He celebrated this joyous occasion by distributing sweets to his colleagues and prominently placing a charming photo of Rishi in his cabin. Many of his close friends and colleagues had already visited him at home, including the CEO, John. The remaining people used this opportunity to greet him personally in the office.

In the afternoon, a meeting of the Apex Thinktank, chaired by the CEO John, was planned. Other members were HR Head Victor, Finance Head Thomas, Quality Head Felix, and Aryan, who was also the convenor of the Thinktank.

John began the meeting by congratulating Aryan on becoming a father and remarked that little Rishi exuded a divine presence with his golden aura. *John also expressed satisfaction in sharing the company's excellent unaudited financial results for FY2022-23.* ***He highlighted how the daily morning ten-minute voluntary meditation sessions, initiated at the behest of Aryan, fostered a harmonious and spiritual work environment, leading to improvement in productivity.*** *The members acknowledged the positive impact of meditation with more cohesive working and negligible instances of heated arguments. Victor added meditation to the training programs, which had a positive influence.*

The Apex group appreciated the previous year's achievements and discussed the challenges for FY2023-24 to prepare for the same. The meeting concluded positively with a message: ***"We must actively drive change to achieve perfection."***

After the inspiring meeting, Aryan returned home early as Dr. Markesic planned to visit them at 5 PM. The conversation began with little Rishi in Shruti's lap, smiling happily upon her arrival. After some time, Shruti's mother brought hot pakoras and tea to relish the discussions. **Dr. Markesic inquired how they nurtured their son as a Corporate Guru in the womb. She also asked about Aryan's role in evolving his company's vision and how Shruti could contribute.**

Aryan said that as the chief learning officer and convenor of Apex Thinktank, he had an essential role in developing and implementing the new initiatives in his financial MNC. The Thinktank thoroughly reviews every new initiative before approving it and seeks the views of other top management team members democratically to incorporate improvements, if any. Aryan elaborated on his pivotal role as he chaired the Young Thinktank, which evolved the primary idea to develop a new initiative. Young Thinktank brainstorms and works on new ideas to create proposals for the Apex Thinktank's review. They usually collaborated with relevant functions during the process.

Dr. Markesic praised Young Thinktank's contributions as she met them twice during Saturday group meditation sessions. She appreciated Aryan's significant contribution to his company in forming strategies and was keen to learn about Shruti's support for them. Shruti explained that even before conceiving, Aryan and Shruti usually meditated together, even when she was far away in Chicago, and they connected telepathically. During her maternity leave, they focused on Rishi's spiritual

Empower Limitless Vision

development through the couple's daily one-hour morning and evening meditation and discussions about Aryan's office activities. During these discussions, they brainstormed new ideas and initiatives, followed by their evening meditation. Sometimes, they receive intuition during meditation to resolve complexities. Aryan often incorporated her suggestions into the proposal for review by Apex Thinktank. She believed this provided valuable insights to their son in the womb to become a Corporate Guru. Aryan praised Shruti for her selfless contributions.

Dr. Markesic was captivated by the couple's bond and looked at little Rishi, who seemed to understand all this and was smiling. Regarding her query about the evolution of his company's vision, Aryan recounted an Apex Thinktank meeting where they initially struggled but later relished the fruits of collective wisdom. He quoted Steve Jobs,

"Your work is going to fill a large part of your life, and the only way to be truly satisfied is to do what you believe is great work. The only way to do great work is to love what you do. If you haven't found it yet, keep looking."

Instead of reinventing the wheel, they explored established approaches and formulated a new strategy for the company's vision by integrating their collective knowledge.

McKinsey 7-S Model

In the subsequent Apex Thinktank meeting, Victor introduced the McKinsey 7-S model as a diagnostic tool for optimizing organizational effectiveness. This model, an evolved iteration of the original 7-S framework by Tom Peters and Robert Waterman, gained fame in their bestselling book, "In Search of Excellence: Lessons from

Empower Limitless Vision

America's Best-Run Companies" (1982), becoming a widely recognized strategic planning tool.

Victor delved into the model's components, categorizing them into **three "Hard Ss" (Strategy, Structure, and Systems) and four "Soft Ss" (Style, Staff, Skills, and Shared Values/Superordinate Goal)**. He stressed the equal importance of all seven elements, emphasizing the need for alignment to achieve breakthroughs. The model's visual representation symbolizes this alignment requirement, with significant progress tied to correct alignment. Victor highlighted that changes in one area necessitate corresponding adjustments elsewhere. The 7-S model is invaluable for performance enhancement, understanding strategic factors, realigning strategies, and assessing overall organizational design. The components of the 7-S model are as follows:

Strategy: Strategy is the foundation for defining organizational goals, prioritizing critical success factors, and outlining actions for achievement. Reliance Industries in India exemplifies strategic success by focusing on thinking big, long-term planning, minimizing competition, and capturing market share with innovative products and services at competitive prices. Successful companies often organize *'Top Management Strategy Meets'* to formulate annual plans based on stakeholder feedback and address business environment challenges.

Structure: Structure ensures alignment with strategy, requiring a transparent chain of command and flexible adaptability with well-defined roles and responsibilities. For instance, MNCs maintain collaboration flexibility while having a tight structure for core operations to protect their niche. Some companies create informal structures to brainstorm initiatives before incorporating them into systems.

<u>**Systems:**</u> Systems should be effective, efficient, and supportive of the strategy. Identifying areas for improvement, especially in "Measurement Parameters," is crucial for success. For example, companies often fail to evolve the _Motivational Metrics_ in performance appraisal and strategy implementation.

<u>**Style:**</u> The leadership style within the organization should align with the strategy and support the shared values or the work culture. Working on _Opportunities for Improvement_ is essential for success. Automobile manufacturers follow a style of _Root Cause Analysis_ for problem-solving and effective supply chain management.

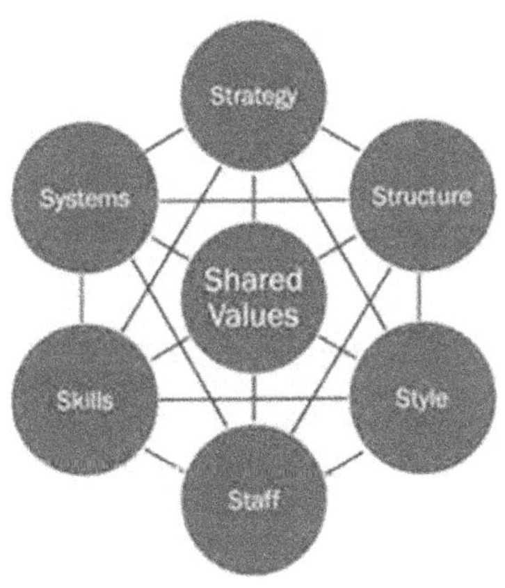

The McKinsey 7-S Model
(Developed by Tom Peters, Robert Waterman, and Julien Philips)

<u>**Staff:**</u> The right people in the right roles are crucial for an organization. For Japanese companies, identifying skill gaps and empowering workers to innovate and implement improvement ideas through building a learning environment with participative management tools like

Kaizen, Quality Circles, Suggestions, etc., is essential for growth. These are now being adopted across the world.

<u>Skills</u>: Skills and knowledge alignment with the organization's strategy is vital. Addressing any skill gaps should be done by providing training and development opportunities. For example, TCS invests significantly in employee well-being and learning, while Apple focuses on up-to-date product knowledge and technical excellence.

<u>Shared Values (Superordinate Goal)</u>: Shared values at the core of the 7-S Model define organizational culture. Staff behavior must embody these values, ensuring alignment with the business strategy. For example, Apple's culture revolves around design and user experience. Indian PSU, BHEL, was driven to success with their initiative - ***'Grahak Safal - Hum Safal'*** (Customer Success is Our Success).

Victor concluded that considering and addressing these seven components empowers organizations to strive for improvement and enhance overall performance. Clear communication of changes to the staff and ensuring their full engagement is crucial for successful implementation.

John, an avid reader and learner, shared the remarks made by Rajat Gupta, former managing director of McKinsey, in a workshop 26 years after introducing this model. Gupta stated,

'The science of management continues to evolve as scholars and global business leaders refine their approaches to organizing their enterprises for profitability and sustainability. While there is no one-size-fits-all solution for business success, I have consistently found that the 7-S framework offers a sound approach by combining all the essential factors that sustain strong organizations: strategy, systems, structure, skills, style, and staff—united by shared values".

Tom Peters, the framework's author, echoed Gupta's sentiments three years later, underscoring the framework's holistic and enduring nature. He concluded, _**"Hard (Strategy, Structure, Systems) is Soft. Soft (Style, Staff, Skills, Shared values) is Hard."**_

Business Excellence Models

Felix, Head of Quality, presented Business Excellence Models and added another dimension to the discussion. Drawing on his experience in European and American MNCs, Felix highlighted the similarities between the European EFQM model and the USA's Baldrige Award, both serving as frameworks for systematic performance excellence.

These models evaluate organizations comprehensively, assessing world-class practices and fundamental business excellence principles. _The Baldrige Award, utilized in over 25 Western countries, consists of six Approach criteria: Leadership, Strategic Planning, Customer and Market Focus, Measurement, Analysis, Knowledge Management, Workforce Focus, and Process Management, and one Results criterion - Business Results._

The European Foundation for Quality Management (EFQM) model, employed by over 30,000 companies in Europe and other regions, comprises five Enablers criteria: Leadership, Policy and Strategy, People, Partnerships and Resources, and Processes, along with four Results criteria: Customer Results, People Results, Society Results, and Key Performance Results.

Business excellence models offer frameworks for organizations to pursue systematic and structured performance excellence. These models encompass all areas and dimensions of an organization, effectively evaluating the adoption of world-class practices and fundamental principles of business excellence. They have been developed and repeatedly refined through extensive study of the methods and values of high-performing organizations worldwide.

Felix emphasized the importance of a compelling vision, stressing effective communication to turn it into reality. Thomas emphasized excellence's essence: "creating value for all stakeholders, including customers, employees, suppliers, partners, shareholders, government entities, and society. Striking a balance between the needs and expectations of these stakeholders is paramount to achieving success and fostering a sustainable strategy. Much like we manage finances to ensure the contentment of all parties, **maintaining a steady 'FLOW' is essential for ushering in excellence**."

John, building upon Thomas's insight about the equilibrium between stakeholder interests and "FLOW," metaphorically likened it to walking a tightrope. He stressed that this balancing act requires exceptional poise and coordination, akin to a performer gracefully traversing the rope while securely clutching a pole. Aryan concluded by relating the bar in this balancing act to 'shared values' or organizational culture. Finally, the Apex Thinktank formulated a flexible approach for broader management group discussion, emphasizing adaptability to changing circumstances.

Approach to Drive the Change

1. <u>Establish a Clear and Shared Vision</u>:

   - Develop ambitious goals and an inspirational vision.
   - Communicate the vision effectively from top management to all employees.

- Organize a workshop for setting specific goals aligned with the Vision.

2. <u>Drive Change as a Catalyst</u>:

   - Act as a catalyst for positive change within the organization and society.
   - Create role models exemplifying Shared Values and the desired Style.
   - Support team aspirations aligned with the organizational vision and values.

3. <u>Foster a Learning Mindset</u>:

   - Embrace a culture of continuous learning.
   - Motivate employees dedicated to quality, productivity, and innovation.
   - Develop new skills as necessary to achieve goals.

4. <u>Foster Collaboration</u>:

   - Collaborate within and outside the organization.
   - Partner with like-minded individuals/organizations.
   - Leverage collective strengths for excellence.

5. <u>Embrace Innovation</u>:

   - Create a structure and systems encouraging innovation.
   - Foster a culture where employees can experiment and improve through group activities.
   - Implement ideas through concepts like Kaizen.

6. <u>Mindful Impact</u>:

   - Examine proposed actions for organizational, social, and environmental impact.
   - Be conscious of consequences and take preventive measures.

- Adopt a proactive approach toward social well-being and environmental sustainability.

7. <u>Continual Measurement</u>:

- Regularly monitor progress toward top leaders' goals.
- Make necessary course corrections within the mentioned points.
- Ensure meaningful progress and timely achievement of the vision.

Aryan wrapped up the discussion by emphasizing the collaborative effort with Shruti, drawing inspiration from the teachings of Himalayan Sadhu. ***Their steadfast belief resided in the harmonization of spirituality and the cosmic laws, encompassing nature's physical and moral laws, ultimately leading to the inevitable attainment of success.*** The aim was to ignite a global transformation movement from the USA, followed by India and other countries. The approach bore the promise of creating a constructive ripple effect within his organization and the broader global community. Dr. Markesic admired the profound insights they had besides the deep love between Aryan and Shruti. She appreciated Shruti's contributions to Aryan's accomplishments and acknowledged Aryan's goodwill at his workplace. The conversation provided valuable input for her research. Aryan generously provided her with a copy of his notes. They planned to meet again every week after Saturday's group meditation sessions for further discussions.

-x-

Evolve a Shared Vision

"Next to doing the right thing, the most important thing is to let people know you are doing the right thing."
— John D. Rockefeller.

At the close of a bustling week, Aryan and Shruti were brimming with joy and contentment as the weekend arrived. They visited Dr. Shweta's Nursing Home for Rishi's vaccination and routine checkup the following week. Four weeks old, Rishi had never shed a tear since his birth, which usually amazed everyone. His radiant smile seemed to emanate divinity eternally. His cherubic countenance had a magnetic quality, captivating passersby and prompting smiles as if drawing down a divine blessing upon them.

Shruti invited Dr. Shweta, Dr. Markesic, Sophia, and Nancy to join them for Saturday's meditation, breakfast, and lunch. Dr. Shweta humbly refused due to some preoccupation, while others agreed to come. Shruti thought that Sophia and Nancy might enrich the ongoing discussions and provide ample opportunity to address Dr. Markesic's inquiries, following their routine group meditation at home.

Relishing her new role as Masi (maternal aunt) to little Rishi, Nancy felt connected even deeper with the family and arrived early to support Shruti in the kitchen. A warm and heartfelt embrace sealed their connection as Shruti whispered, "I sense a profound bond as if we were sisters in a past life." In response, Nancy shared a quote by Chris Hart, "All the statistics in the world can't measure the warmth of a smile." Their camaraderie transcended the boundaries of their present lives as if their souls had intertwined through multiple lifetimes. The warmth of their collective presence was palpable.

Aryan, slightly tired, roused himself a bit later and prepared for the group meditation at 9 a.m. Nancy, too, arrived early and met with the charming Sophia. She was embracing her newfound role as Bua (paternal aunt) to Rishi. Sophia swiftly took charge of adorning the meditation room, supported by other members of the Young Thinktank. The group meditation unfolded like the previous week, concluding with participants leaving with radiant faces. Rishi, nestled in Shruti's lap, had a way of augmenting their sense of spirituality.

Post-meditation, they shared tea and cookies, basking in the delight of the memorable moments that had unfolded since Rishi's birth at the end of March. With May Day approaching the following week, none seemed interested in it. Their lively conversations spanned various topics, including meditation experiences, office intricacies, and social gossip.

Following breakfast, Dr. Markesic, Sophia, Aryan, and Shruti gathered in the drawing room. Meanwhile, Nancy opted to join Shruti's mother indoors, where Rishi was napping in another room. Shruti kept a watchful eye on her son with the CCTV feed on her mobile device.

After finalizing the approach to drive excellence, Aryan discussed it with Shruti, seeking her valuable insights. She highlighted the importance of functional coordinators for support, progress monitoring, and seamless implementation. Aryan assured her that the Young Thinktank would manage this aspect effectively. Shruti also suggested evolving and incorporating the company's values into functional polestars. Sophia confirmed that both points raised by Shruti had been addressed, unaware that Shruti was the originator of these ideas. Aryan and Shruti exchanged smiles as they listened to Sophia.

In the first week of February, Aryan facilitated a one-day top management workshop at the Lodge at Woodloch in Pennsylvania, located in the Pocono Mountains, a 2.5-hour drive from New York, with support from Sophia and the Young Thinktank. To manage logistics, Aryan reached the venue a day before the workshop, while others came on the workshop day. ***Aryan, while meditating early in the morning on the workshop day, had a mystical experience. He felt the presence of the Himalayan Sadhu amidst nature's serenity, offering him deeper self-understanding.***

Aryan presented the approach finalized by the Apex Thinktank for discussion by the participants. Participants unanimously adopted this strategy without any change. The first step to implementing the strategy was to evolve the company's vision.

John said, *"Let us dream big and create an inspirational vision, establish its common understanding, and set specific goals."*

Aryan presented the vision of some leading companies and competitors, but it didn't resonate with the participants' thoughts. There was a stalemate. During lunch, John privately discussed the post-lunch strategy with Thomas. Simultaneously, Victor and Felix noticed Aryan, Sophia, and Young Thinktank were nervous. Drawing upon their rich experience, they encouraged them and suggested Aryan change the seating arrangement. When the post-lunch session began, the seating arrangement surprised participants. This change staggered the seats of the Apex Thinktank members, who were earlier sitting together, into the' U' shape. It helped to build positive group dynamics.

Empower Limitless Vision

Beginning the post-lunch session, John suggested, "Let's go back to the basics. Vision refers to a mental image or a dream we wish to realize. So, let's define what we wish to accomplish in the coming 3 to 5 years." Participants agreed with him.

He continued, *"A vision should clearly show a better future. It is essential for success. A vision should create a sense of purpose, set direction and measurable goals, and provide a roadmap to achieve those goals. It should be inspirational to motivate employees to associate their aspirations with it. Vision is an important component of strategic planning."* Everyone agreed with his perspective.

Sitting on the other side of the 'U' shape, Thomas said, "Let's review the vision statements presented earlier and identify the key points for our vision." Felix and Victor, sitting on opposite sides in the 'U' shape, supported his views. It motivated others to agree.

Explore the Vision of Leading Companies

Aryan once again shared the vision statements presented earlier in alphabetic order to avoid any bias and requested participants to find key points in each statement. He asked Sophia to note keywords emerging from the discussion on a whiteboard. The Visions presented were:

- **Amazon:** "To be *Earth's most customer-centric company,* where customers can find and *discover anything* they want to buy online."
- **American Express:** "To become the *world's most respected* service brand."
- **Apple:** "To make a *contribution to the world* by making tools for the mind that *advance humankind.*"
- **Goldman Sachs:** "To be the leading *global* investment banking, securities, and investment management firm."

Empower Limitless Vision

- **Google:** "To organize the *world's information* and make it *universally accessible* and useful."
- **Infosys:** "To be a *globally respected* corporation that provides *best-of-breed business solutions*, leveraging technology, delivered by *best-in-class people*."
- **JPMorgan:** "We aim to be the *most respected financial services* firm in the world, serving corporations and individuals in more than 100 countries."
- **Mahindra:** "To *drive positive change* in the lives of our stakeholders and *communities across the world*, to enable them to Rise."
- **Microsoft:** "*Empower* every person and every organization *on the planet* to achieve more."
- **Reliance Industries:** "To be a *leading* provider of superior *quality* products and services at *competitive prices*, to give our customers an *unparalleled experience*, and *maximize value* for all our stakeholders."
- **Tata:** "To improve the *quality of life* of the communities we serve *globally through long-term stakeholder value* creation based on *Leadership with Trust*."
- **Toyota:** "To be the *most respected and admired company*."
- **Walmart:** "To *save people money* so they can *live better*."
- **Wipro:** "To be a *world-class, innovative,* and integrated IT & BPO services provider, delivering *sustainable value to all stakeholders*."

The participants discussed and suggested vital points from each presented vision statement. Some of these points were repetitive and similar. John instructed Sophia to jot down all issues on the Board to facilitate a free flow of ideas. His approach proved successful, fostering a sense of involvement in the vision evolution process and satisfying egos.

Despite the fast-paced idea generation, Sophia attempted to arrange similar points together, resulting in the division of the ideas under the following keywords:

1. **Think global**: Emphasize becoming a global brand, earning respect and trust from stakeholders, promoting integrity and ethical conduct, and aiming to be the world's most respected and admired company, with a focus on being world-class and universally accessible while empowering the planet.

2. **Customer satisfaction**: Highlight conveying the company's values, eliminating suffering for stakeholders, offering best-of-breed business solutions, providing superior quality at competitive prices, delivering an unparalleled customer experience, maximizing value, saving people money, offering innovative solutions, establishing strong relationships with clients, and being recognized as Earth's most customer-centric company.

3. **Social responsibility**: Emphasize making a positive impact on the world, preserving the planet, advancing humankind, and improving the quality of life in communities.

4. **Big dream**: Define a clear direction and unique aspiration, focus on niche areas, be an inspiring company, contribute to the world, drive positive change, serve communities worldwide, create long-term stakeholder value, and provide sustainable value to all stakeholders.

5. **Employee Focus**: Highlight the goal of attracting and retaining the best talent, having a workforce of best-in-class people, and establishing leadership with trust.

Empower Limitless Vision

6. **<u>Others</u>**: Emphasize brevity, simplicity, and easy understanding, as well as wisdom.

After a long and productive brainstorming, it was getting late, and the participants were still engrossed in discussions and didn't want to lose momentum. Participants suggested that the snacks be served on the table and that the time be extended.

Victor suggested Aryan divide the participants into four groups to draft a vision statement in 30 minutes. Meanwhile, the resort team served the snacks to the participants in four groups. Sophia and the young team actively participated in the groups while CEO John separately discussed the next steps with Aryan to finalize the Vision. The four groups shared their drafted vision statements for discussion and refinement into a final vision for the company. The resulting vision statement evolved:

"To be an ethical company committed to the well-being of mankind providing world-class financial services globally."

CEO John thanked everyone for their contribution to evolving the company's Vision and suggested sharing it with employees and other stakeholders for their feedback within 15 days. The Apex Thinktank would review any necessary changes in the vision based on input received and share it with the top management team.

Aryan, Sophia, and the Young Thinktank were praised for adaptability and proactive problem-solving, highlighting the importance of collaboration. The leadership's commitment to transparency was visible from active participation and seeking feedback, ensuring wide acceptance of the resulting vision statement.

Empower Limitless Vision

At home, Aryan explained everything in detail to Shruti and answered her pointed questions as both were inspired to ensure their son learned all these complexities in his mother's womb.

Dr. Markesic, Sophia, and Nancy were amazed to know about the meticulous planning Aryan and Shruti did for their son. After an elegant and tasteful lunch, they bid farewell. On Sunday, Aryan, Shruti, Shruti's mother, and Rishi enjoyed a long drive in the sunny winter weather, returning late in the evening.

-x-

Empower Limitless Vision

Inspire the Change

"Drive the change within yourself, for only through personal transformation can the world be truly transformed."   - Rigveda.

Dr. Markesic admired Aryan's deep knowledge of Hinduism, spirituality, and ancient wisdom, areas she rarely explored during her occasional Church visits. Acknowledging her limited exposure to religious insights, she refrained from comparing religions, as did Aryan, who focused on individual learning and insights. Dr. Markesic, maintaining her role as a neutral researcher, revisited their home to learn about activities during the eighth and ninth months of Shruti's pregnancy, aiming to nurture her son into a corporate monk.

Coincidentally, Aryan's childhood friend, Ramesh, was present during this visit. Initially indifferent to meditation, Ramesh became intrigued as he listened to Dr. Markesic's questions and enlightening insights from Aryan and Shruti. Ramesh proposed streamlining the research by integrating it with weekly group meditation. They deliberated and decided to continue with the Saturday morning meditation session from 9 a.m. for 45 minutes as earlier, followed by a 15-minute refreshment break. Participants may voluntarily bring pure vegetarian prasad from their homes and place it on a designated table. Aryan's home would provide self-service tea, and after refreshments, Dr. Markesic would ask research-related queries, with Aryan and Shruti responding. Any group meditation participant interested in the conversation may join the 90-minute session as a listener. Ramesh volunteered to distribute any leftover vegetarian offerings to devotees at the nearby Ganesha temple. They decided to begin the new arrangement the following Saturday.

Accordingly, Dr. Markesic and Ramesh brought vegetarian Prasad and informed participants about the changes on Saturday. Most participants appreciated this new arrangement.

The Model for Happiness

Three weeks later, during a subsequent session, Dr. Markesic inquired about the participant's response to the new arrangement. The unanimous expression was happiness. Aryan elucidated that it aligned with the happiness model, which he expressed mathematically as:

Happiness=Reality–Expectations

Participants in meditation had no expectations for Prasad, and their contributions were voluntary. Hence, reality surpassed expectations, leading to happiness. Aryan quoted *Lord Krishna's teachings in the Bhagavad Gita, emphasizing performing Karma without expecting results. This profound ancient wisdom suggested that any outcome surpassing expectations brings happiness. Similarly, Jesus Christ advocated helping the needy, aligning with these thoughts.*

Dr. Markesic's question prompted a participant to ask about the difference between Eastern and Western religious beliefs. Aryan likened these beliefs to two streams of water merging into a common destination. He cited Swami Vivekananda's speech at the 1893 World Parliament of Religions:

'As different streams, having their sources in different places, all mingle their water in the sea, so, O Lord, the different paths which men take through different tendencies, various though they appear, crooked or straight, all lead to Thee.'

Empower Limitless Vision

Aryan described how his joint meditation practice with Shruti created synchronicity and revitalized their pranic energy. The couple recognized the multifaceted benefits of daily meditation, and engaging in meditation and pranayama together amplified the rewards. This routine kept them vibrant and healthy and exuded a natural radiance that captivated those around them. Significantly, these practices profoundly benefited their child in the womb.

At the office, Aryan and the functional coordinators initiated an online survey to gather feedback on the company's vision statement, which was formulated in a top management workshop. Young Thinktank members assumed functional roles, with Sophia overseeing overall coordination. Within a week, they consolidated feedback from 30 percent of employees and presented the findings to the Apex Thinktank. The feedback indicated that while the employees understood the vision statement, they lacked clarity about its implementation.

After the presentation, CEO John commended the team and praised Sophia for her facilitation skills. Sophia credited Aryan's leadership and the collaborative effort of Young Thinktank. Finance Head Thomas acknowledged Aryan's trust in the team through empowerment, aligning individual aspirations with the company's vision. John concluded that the first "S" of the McKinsey 7-S Model, Shared Vision, was already in place, and the remaining six "S" were to be addressed. The feedback indicated that 4-S required attention: Style, Staff, Skills, and Shared Values. They agreed on fostering collaboration, empowering subordinates, embracing challenges, and addressing social and environmental issues.

Empower Limitless Vision

Functional Polestar

John acknowledged Aryan's exceptional organizational skills and welcomed his ideas for long-term change, particularly the latest concept of the Functional Polestar. Apex Thinktank approved the proposal for developing the Functional Polestar, which aligned with the company's vision as an effective strategy. The Finance Function was designated to initiate this work, and the Apex Thinktank meeting concluded on a positive note.

After approval, Aryan convened a meeting of Functional Coordinators — Robin from Finance, James from Marketing, Adam from Technology, Emma from HR, and Hanna from Planning. Sophia, working with Aryan, was the overall coordinator. The coordinators, though enthusiastic, were apprehensive about evolving functional visions.

Aryan assigned them to organize brainstorming sessions in their respective areas. He emphasized that the power of mantras lies in their sacred sounds formed by syllables. Just as a remedy or medicine needs its root or source to be effective, mantras cannot exist without syllables. Aryan shared an ancient hymn,

"There is no letter without a charisma, no root without a medicinal property, no incompetent person exists, but a competent organizer is rare." – An ancient hymn.

He highlighted that everyone possesses unique talents, but finding a competent organizer is rare. The coordinators' role was to be catalysts and planners, ensuring effective resource utilization. Robin initially took the lead in organizing the Finance function's brainstorming session.

With the year-end work pressure increasing daily, John asked Aryan to complete the exercise by mid-March.

Empower Limitless Vision

Internally, Aryan was happy with this schedule, as March would be the ninth month of Shruti's pregnancy, and they may teach their child in the womb some challenging learnings from the exercise.

In collaboration, Aryan and Shruti realized that deriving Functional Polestars from the company's overarching vision wouldn't motivate and engage employees. They meditated and prayed for divine bliss and guidance. During meditation, Aryan envisioned Goddess Lakshmi blessing him with profound wisdom, aligning the Finance Function's vision with her virtues. In this moment of deep connection, a ray of light passed through his spine. It sparked creative ideas that the visions for other functions may be developed by connecting their goals with Hindu mythology's virtues of related Gods and Goddesses.

Simultaneously, Shruti meditated and envisioned the divine ***"Trinity" – Brahma, Vishnu, and Shiva.*** However, she couldn't initially correlate this intuition with any specific business operation. In a subsequent meditation, she experienced a vision of the universe emerging from the Trinity, merging into the sacred symbol of OM. This vision aligned with Vedanta teachings and emphasized the interdependence of the Trinity's powers. Recognizing that the Trinity embodies "Shared Values," Shruti concluded that these values are vital for success.

Aryan and Shruti contemplated that businesses should adopt Shared Values from the Trinity, deriving Functional Polestars from the divine. They identified corporate roles analogous to the Hindu Trinity —Brahma, Vishnu, and Shiva — attributed to different organizational elements or individuals.

Creation (Brahma) - Founder, Initiate New Business: Lord Brahma, the creator of the universe, in a corporate context, aligns to initiating new businesses,

Empower Limitless Vision

investments, products, projects, ventures, designs, employee recruitment, new ideas, and innovations. It encompasses conceiving new concepts, building strategies, identifying opportunities, and formulating business plans to bring new initiatives to life. The entrepreneur or company founder often embodies this role, setting the initial direction and value system. CEOs and their teams take on this role as the company evolves, envisioning innovative offerings rooted in its Shared Values to drive growth.

Sustenance (Vishnu) - Board of Directors, Operational Excellence: Mirroring Vishnu, the preserver of the universe in the corporate context, is responsible for maintaining and nourishing the corporate body throughout its existence. The Board of Directors is pivotal in preserving the company's long-term interests. They oversee the strategy, ensure regulatory compliance, and safeguard sustainability and ethical practices. Various teams and departments responsible for planning, supply chain management, processes, quality, finance, customer service, and human resources contribute to sustaining and preserving daily operations. They align day-to-day working with ethical practices and the organization's Shared Values.

Transformation (Shiva) – Monitoring, Law Enforcement, Change Management: Embodied by Lord Shiva, this role in corporates signifies the power of transformation and renewal to remain competitive and relevant. Shiva enforces laws, values, systems, audits, assessments, and appraisals to gain new insights for sustainability, business transformation, and closure. Independent Directors, Investors, and bankers play this role in examining progress and suggesting measures for excellence. It involves strategies for change management, innovation, and continuous improvement. Corporations must be capable of restructuring, rebranding, and adapting when needed. Government monitoring and law enforcement agencies act as agents of Shiva, intervening to enforce compliance, investigate irregularities, and facilitate changes aligned with the organization's Shared Values. Internal audits, self-assessment, and change management teams contribute to transformation while ensuring adaptability to evolving market conditions.

Aryan concluded they realized that no single department within a company assumes all three roles of the Trinity. Instead, the teams, departments, and leaders collectively embody these aspects, ensuring growth, stability, and adaptability in a dynamic business environment. Shared Values remain at the heart of this approach, fostering a synergetic relationship in the corporate world. It enables businesses to create opportunities, sustain their operations effectively, and be ready for renewal and transformation. This holistic approach helps organizations achieve long-term success and resilience in the turbulent business landscape.

Sophia exclaimed. Oh! So, this was the inside story of your meeting with the CEO to evolve Shared Values for the company before finalizing Functional Polestars.

Dr. Markesic was satisfied with her research inputs and was keen to know how the Shared Values evolved. Thus, they set the agenda for their meeting next Saturday.

-x-

Inculcate Shared Values

"Everything in the universe, including the universe itself, is in motion, inhabited, permeated, surrounded, or embraced by God. Choose to enjoy a renounced existence, abstaining from coveting anyone else's wealth." — *Yajur Veda 40/1*

The following Saturday, Aryan, Shruti, her mother, Dr. Markesic, and attendees Ramesh, Nancy, and Sophia engaged in post-meditation discussions. Aryan continued sharing his journey of nurturing his son as a Corporate Guru, unveiling the evolution of Shared Values. As the other participants left for their homes after the meditation session, Shruti extended an invitation for lunch, arranging Indian restaurant delivery.

Aryan recounted his subsequent meeting with CEO John, where he proposed a significant shift in the corporate strategy. He suggested prioritizing establishing and embracing shared values before developing Functional Polestars for the company. Drawing from insights gained during meditation sessions with Shruti, Aryan highlighted the importance of human values deeply rooted in Indian mythology.

Emphasizing that Indian mythology recognizes sixteen dimensions of excellence in human life, with legendary figures serving as role models, Aryan cited *Lord Rama's excellence in 14 dimensions (14 Kala Sampuran) and Lord Krishna's mastery in all 16 dimensions (16 Kala Sampuran).* These dimensions, grounded in human values, have been central in scriptures, promoting sustainable growth and overall well-being.

Empower Limitless Vision

Referencing academic research by Chakraborty (1995), Saraswat (2005), Gustavsson et al. (1996), and Bourne et al. (2005), Aryan underscored the critical role of human values as a differentiator for organizational success. Impressed by Aryan's past contributions and convincing mythological references, CEO John readily acknowledged the significance of Shared Values in the 7-S McKinsey model. He entrusted Aryan with organizing the Apex Thinktank meeting to present a blueprint of Shared Values.

Aryan promptly gathered the Young Thinktank for a meeting and assigned various responsibilities. He delegated Sophia to inform Apex Thinktank members about the upcoming session and collect information on Core Values from different Business Excellence Models, seeking guidance from Felix. He asked other Thinktank members to explore and consolidate insights on human values for a presentation during the Apex Thinktank meeting. Aryan himself took on the responsibility of delving into scriptures, especially the Bhagavad Gita, to identify and understand its articulated human values.

In the evening, Aryan shared the day's outcomes with Shruti. Shruti was pleased that John had agreed to evolve and implement Shared Values promptly. They discussed potential Shared Values for the company, drawing inspiration from the intuition of the Trinity during their meditation. Shruti proposed that Brahma, representing creation, could inspire a Value focused on promoting new ideas and an instinct for growth. Aryan agreed, adding that Shiva, symbolizing self-restraint and managing transformation, could contribute to another Value. They concluded that Vishnu, as the preserver, could underpin a value that promotes operational excellence. Recognizing the importance of honesty and integrity for organizational continuity, they considered these virtues integral. This discussion gave Aryan a guiding framework for the upcoming Apex Thinktank meeting.

Empower Limitless Vision

Two days later, at the outset of the Apex Thinktank meeting, CEO John clarified the purpose of the meeting: identifying Shared Values for the company before developing Functional Polestars. He emphasized that Values were actions upheld right in the past, present, and future, stressing the need for measures that safeguard the broader interests of humanity and positively impact society. With these opening remarks, he handed over the presentation to Aryan.

Aryan began his presentation by introducing a three-part structure. Sophia will present the first part on the core values of business excellence models, while Robin and Hanna will jointly cover the second part on human values. Aryan would then deliver the third part, marking a groundbreaking moment as the Young Thinktank members presented a conceptual idea to the Apex group for the first time. The extensive involvement of the Young Thinktank pleasantly surprised the Apex group.

Core Values of Business Excellence Models

Sophia initiated her presentation by highlighting her thorough study of three highly regarded models advised by Felix and used by numerous corporations worldwide: the Deming Prize of Japan, the Malcolm Baldrige National Quality Award (MBNQA) of the USA, and the European Foundation for Quality Management (EFQM) model. Felix also advised her to explore other models if time permits. She studied *sixteen National Quality Awards/Business Excellence models, including models from Japan, Singapore, Canada, Australia, the UK, and more. This comprehensive research led to the compilation of an exhaustive list of twenty core values:*

1. Leadership and Constancy of Purpose

2. Customer Focus / Quality

Empower Limitless Vision

3. Continuous Learning, Innovation & Improvement

4. Employee Engagement & Development

5. Partnership Development

6. Agility

7. Focus on the Future

8. Social Responsibility

9. Focus on Results and Creating Value

10. Systems, Processes, and Facts-based Management

11. Cooperation/Teamwork/Faster Response

12. Cease Mass Inspection / Understand Variation

13. Eliminate Numerical Quotas

14. Eliminate Slogans

15. Vigorous Education, Training, and Retraining

16. Knowledge Management

17. Organizational and Personal Learning

18. Globalization

19. Fairness

20. Drive Out Fear

She noted that, at their core, these fundamental values are Business Values, stemming from the Human Values promoted by social scientists and religious teachings. Felix commended Sophia for her efforts within a tight timeframe, emphasizing that adherence to human values inherently leads to adopting most of the core values of excellence models. However, the reverse is not always true. In an extensive literature review covering over 300 research papers, the author identified limited research efforts incurred to integrate these models with Human Values.

Empower Limitless Vision

'Human Values' – Way to Sustainable Success

The second segment of the presentation, led by Robin from Finance and Hanna from Planning, explored the integration of Human Values based on their examination of research papers. Some researchers advocated for companies to revive and adopt value systems reminiscent of pre-industrial societies, encouraging the free expression of divine instincts and mirroring Aryan experiences. *The human values outlined in the sixteenth chapter of the Bhagavad Gita are a testament to this ancient wisdom.* ***The corporate world needs a "Corporate Guru" to impart wisdom on Market Karma, Social Dharma, and Leadership Charisma to enhance humanity's material and spiritual conditions.***

In his best-seller "The Fortune at the Bottom of the Pyramid," C.K. Prahalad asserted that viewing people experiencing poverty as resilient and creative entrepreneurs and value-conscious consumers could unlock new opportunities. Chakraborty (1995) endorsed the superconscious insights of sages from sacred religious literature as the foundation of ethical, social, and other human values, underlining their universal humanistic nature.

Saraswat (2005) identified fourteen principles of Human Values from the Bhagavad Gita, including fearlessness, purity of thoughts, pursuit of knowledge, charity, self-control, noble and selfless work, self-study, disciplined living, compassion, non-violence, truthfulness, tranquillity, friendliness, and humility. Marsh and Conley (1999) identified vital concepts like honesty, trust, and commitment to quality and service. Several other academicians, including Anderson (1997), Becker (1998), and Putnam (1993), endorsed the importance of practicing Human Values. They identified trust, respect, integrity, harmony, loyalty, justice, and honesty as essential human

Empower Limitless Vision

values and spiritual dimensions necessary to attain excellence.

All members of the Apex Thinktank appreciated the substantial effort put forth by Robin and Hanna, eagerly anticipating Aryan's value addition.

Aryan's presentation delved deeper into the study of ancient wisdom, uncovering valuable insights on practicing Human Values within the Vedic hymns, the Bhagavad Gita, and the Manu-Smriti. For instance, the *Manu-Smriti stressed the supreme importance of purity in earning money, emphasizing the significance of knowledge and justice over monetary gain. Bhagavad Gita says that knowledge and wisdom eliminate fear.* Therefore, creating a learning organization is a must for success. Chanakya Niti advocated adopting an ethical approach and meeting the community's expectations to serve your long-term interests.

Aryan noted that other religious texts also emphasized practicing Values. *Edwards (2004) argued that Christianity in the West was the foundation of the free enterprise economic system, with the profit motive optimally tempered by higher Christian motives.* Contemporary businesses may also apply the commandments to love God with all one's heart, soul, strength, and mind and to love one's neighbor as one loves oneself as one's shared values. These include fiduciary responsibility to investors, profit-making, treatment of employees, outsourcing jobs, and importation of foreign workers. He concludes that a Christian business ethic is superior because its practitioner is principally concerned with the eternal and glorifying God through his conduct in all areas of life, including commerce.

Aryan continued by discussing how researchers argued that workplace spirituality was critical to organizational success. A scientific objectivity independent from traditions is possible in ethical and moral matters. He concluded that incorporating various dimensions of spirituality into the workplace could enhance personal well-being, creativity, organizational harmony, and long-term business success. Alvin Toffler foretold the technological "third wave" in 1980 and suggested that there is an organizational fourth wave, the spiritually-based firm. Aryan wrapped up his presentation by sharing a comprehensive list of 'Human Values' as below:

1. Honesty

2. Integrity and Purity of thoughts

3. Self-restraint – Control of senses

4. Self-learning and Knowledge-sharing

5. Self-discipline

6. Fearlessness

7. Pursuit of knowledge

8. Almsgiving – Giving away in Charity

9. Noble and Selfless work

10. Straightforwardness - Uprightness

11. Non-injuriousness

12. Non-violence

13. Renunciation

14. Peace

15. Absence of fault finding and calumny

16. Compassion and Respect for all beings

17. Non-covetousness (absence of greed)

18. Gentleness

Empower Limitless Vision

19. Modesty

20. Absence of restlessness

21. Radiance of Character - Boldness

22. Justice

23. Patience on fortitude

24. Tranquillity

25. Non-hatred

26. Mutual Trust and Loyalty

27. Lack of conceit - Absence of pride

Emphasizing the power of Human Values, the Quality Head, Felix, highlighted their role in adopting Excellence model values for sustained success. It sparked a conversation among participants. Given recent scandals, the Finance Head stressed the importance of honesty and integrity, while the HR Head underscored the need for transparency in dealings. Felix suggested looking at the approach to drive the change finalized by the Apex group. To drive change and foster collaboration, learner mindset, and innovation, a value could be 'Drive Learning and Innovation.' For mindful impact and continual measurement, a value could be Self-Discipline. John nodded his head in affirmation. **They decided Integrity, Honesty, Transparency, driving learning & innovation, and Self-discipline as the Shared Values for the company.** Aryan was happy as the Apex group addressed all his points without provocation.

Concluding the meeting, John tasked Aryan with a brief presentation on Shared Values in the Top Management team's operations review meeting the next day. Subsequently, the Top Management team unanimously embraced the Shared Values, marking a significant milestone in their excellence journey.

Empower Limitless Vision

With this, Aryan concluded his narration about the Shared Values. Dr. Markesic had some queries, which Aryan answered to windup the discussion. Afterward, everyone enjoyed lunch together, served by Sophia and Nancy. The week passed without significant development, and Dr. Markesic eagerly awaited Saturday to get more input from the blessed couple to complete her project.

-x-

Maternal Influence on Unborn Child

"All that I am, or ever hope to be, I owe to my angel mother." *- Abraham Lincoln.*

Voluntary Prasad distribution after the group meditation gained popularity, becoming a weekly tradition. James, a bachelor participant from the neighborhood, brought sweets for his birthday on May 27 as Prasad. It led to the beginning of a new practice. Now, group meditation includes prayers for the participants celebrating birthdays or anniversaries that week. It transformed the meditation experience into a celebratory and bonding ritual.

James stayed for the post-meditation interactive session led by Dr. Markesic after the meditation session. This week, Dr. Markesic shifted her focus from Aryan to Shruti, inquiring about her experience with maternal influence on the unborn child. Shruti joyfully recounted the meticulous care she and Aryan took to nurture Rishi during pregnancy and after birth. The couple spent countless hours planning each developmental activity, receiving astral divine blessings from Himalayan Sages. Dr. Markesic and other participants were deeply engrossed in understanding their unique journey and the process of instilling divinity in Rishi during pregnancy. Despite Rishi being under two months old, signs of divinity were already reflected in him, showcasing the couple's willingness to sacrifice their bright careers for this cause.

Dr. Markesic specifically asked Shruti about her efforts to instill virtues in Rishi during the eighth and ninth months of pregnancy. Shruti explained that, according to ancient wisdom, this is when a mother can instill desired virtues in her child. Dr. Markesic wanted to create empirical evidence to demonstrate how Aryan and Shruti taught specific values to Rishi. Thus, continuing the inquiry into the shared values of Aryan's company, which they discussed the previous week, she asked Shruti's views on these values.

Shruti was happy with these shared values and associated them with the Trinity. She believed 'Transparency in dealing' is essential to sustain an organization and is linked to Lord Vishnu. 'Learning and Innovation' lead to new creation, development, and growth related to Lord Brahma. Self-discipline is necessary for ethical conduct, avoids forced discipline by enforcement authorities, and is linked to Lord Shiva.

When asked about the essential values for Rishi, Shruti highlighted six values: **gratitude, forgiveness, love, humility, giving without expectations, and patience. Gratitude enhances divine blessings. Forgiveness prevents anger and hatred. Love is transformative wisdom that transforms enemies into friends. Humility is modesty and involves sharing success credit with others. Giving without expectations is like a mother's love. Patience, a virtue of Aryan, is crucial for success.**

Replying to a query about Truth as a Value, she mentioned Swami Dayananda Sarasvati's quest for truth leading to enlightenment and attaining God. **When the truth enlightens your Soul, you attain God.** The clarity of Shruti's thoughts amazed everyone, with James expressing a valuable life lesson learned.

Dr. Markesic inquired about Aryan's next steps after finalizing Shared Values. Aryan discussed the challenge of correlating each function with a deity due to the vastness of the Trinity. Despite limitations, the couple identified key functions of an organization and attempted to link them to Hindu gods or goddesses, aiming to facilitate the evolution of functional Polestars and connect divine virtues with unique skills required for each function.

For instance, the **Finance Function aligns with Goddess Lakshmi, symbolizing Wealth and Prosperity**. Therefore, the functional Polestar for Finance should embody the virtues of Goddess Lakshmi. Like the Goddess, money needs to circulate for prosperity, avoiding blockages such as cash blockage with debtors, excessive inventory in operations, lack of utilization of assets, etc. The blockage in money flow hinders efficiency.

Goddess Lakshmi stays with Lord Vishnu, the preserver of the universe and protector of ethics. Inheriting the virtues of Vishnu enables Lakshmi to remain with the devotee. Similarly, utilizing money for smooth company operations and the well-being of humanity sustains prosperity and enhances the company's goodwill.

Similarly, Lakshmi associates with Lord Ganesha, the God of Wisdom, and 'Pratham Pujya,' the first deity worshipped. Wise investments with holistic planning contribute to growth. Aryan concluded these insights should shape the functional Polestar for the Finance Function.

Expressing admiration, Ramesh exclaimed, "Wonderful! I've never heard such a thoughtful analogy for corporate functions."

Shruti added that it would inspire Finance function employees to learn Goddess Lakshmi's skills. Subsequently, they explored and set the initial foundation for developing functional Polestars for various functions.

Now, Aryan briefly outlined the broad connections between deities and other corporate departments:

- **Ganesha,** the Pratham Pujya, remover of obstacles, and the God of Wisdom may inspire the Functional Polestar of Strategic Planning and Business Intelligence.

- **Bhagwan Rama,** an Avatar of Lord Vishnu and the God of Ethics, could relate to the Functional Polestar of CEO, Human Resources, and Operations.

- **Vishwakarma,** the Celestial Craftsman of the Universe, may be associated with the Functional Polestars of Quality, Excellence, and Manufacturing.

- **Agni,** the God of Fire, symbolizing rapid growth that needs control to prevent losses, may influence the Functional Polestars for Defence, IT, Technology, Cybersecurity, and Sales.

- **Goddess Sarasvati,** the Goddess of Skills, Knowledge, and creativity, could inspire the Functional Polestar of Engineering, Research, Learning, Fine Arts, and HRD.

- **Indra,** the King of the Devas with expertise in multiple areas, might be linked to roles like CEO, Sales and Marketing, Business Development, etc.

- **Varuna,** the God of Water and Cosmic Order, representing constant flow and expansion, may relate to the Functional Polestar of Supply Chain Management, Logistics Flow, and Process Industries like automobile manufacturing lines, refineries, etc.

- **Kubera,** the God of Wealth and Treasure, Head of the invaluable resources of the Universe, may inspire functional areas like Banking, Cash, Stores, and Mines.

- **Hanumana,** the Monkey God and devoted follower of Bhagwan Rama is a problem solver and expert in crisis management. His influence extends to innovation, project management, change management, employee engagement, and establishing a new work culture. Hanumana embodies wisdom, knowledge, bravery, loyalty and serves as an esteemed ambassador of God. Functional Polestars for Projects, Services, Market Intelligence, Internal Security, Police, Investigative agencies, and Foreign Office may align with Him.

- **Surya,** the Sun God, symbolizes profound discipline and the boundless radiance of light and energy. He encompasses illumination, knowledge, vitality, and divine presence. The Functional Polestar for health, environment, essential services, energy, and learning may resonate with Surya's qualities.

- **Chandra,** the Moon God, imparts serenity, coolness, and a reflective aspect of consciousness. Associated with daily fluctuations, Chandra symbolizes the share market, fashion, new products, and environmental changes. The Functional Polestar related to the Fashion industry, Film and Media industry, Sports, New Product launches, and Campaigns serving as the face of the company may align with Chandra.

- **Narada,** a sage divinity renowned as a traveling musician and storyteller in Hindu traditions, carries news and enlightening wisdom. His virtues can be linked to the Functional Polestar of Public Relations, Communications, and Digital Marketing to enhance the company's public image and reputation.

Shruti added that we felt these correlations are symbolic and metaphorical, establishing parallels between the qualities or responsibilities linked to the deities and their closest alignment with a corporate function or an industry. If someone deeply admired a specific God or Goddess, they would be most suited for the work associated with that deity, quickly developing skills and competence in that domain. This correlation could aid in evolving functional visions, identifying competent individuals for the function, and motivating them to align their aspirations with dreams or Polestars.

Armed with this newfound insight, Aryan felt content and resolved to incorporate this knowledge into crafting practical guiding principles and visions for various corporate functions. They envisioned fostering a more profound understanding through brainstorming sessions, believing that this exercise would enhance conceptual clarity and benefit their unborn son, Rishi, who is still in Shruti's womb. Dr. Markesic remarked, "Now I grasp your unique and innovative approach to infusing spirituality in the workplace for its manifold advantages." As they concluded the session, they decided to delve into functional Polestars in their next meeting.

Earlier in the week, Shruti proposed a unique celebration for Rishi's monthly birthday, which falls on Sunday, May 28, by spending time at an orphanage and offering gifts to needy children. Aryan embraced the idea and organized the arrangements for Rishi's second monthly birthday celebration. Shruti invited Dr. Markesic and Ramesh to join them on Sunday before they departed after Saturday's session. Both agreed.

Later, Shruti shared the inside story of her invitation to them with Aryan. Aryan's childhood friend Ramesh had recently started regularly attending the weekly meditations and joined Dr. Markesic's post-meditation research interactions as a thoughtful listener. Shruti silently observed that a liking was developing between Dr. Markesic and Ramesh, but their relationship hadn't progressed. She hoped this invitation might be a breakthrough that would bring them closer and motivate them to spend Sunday evenings together after visiting the orphanage.

On Sunday, May 28, they joyously celebrated Rishi's second monthly milestone with the children at the orphanage in New Jersey. The celebration included cake-cutting, games, and the exchange of gifts, followed by a delightful lunch generously sponsored by Aryan and Shruti. The children were brimming with happiness and gratitude. Aryan and Shruti committed to visiting the orphanage on the 28th day of every month until Rishi becomes one year old.

As they bid farewell to the orphanage after lunch, Shruti proposed to Ramesh to visit the Swaminarayan Mandir in Robbinsville, Central New Jersey, along with Dr. Markesic. It would offer her a deeper understanding of the essence of Hinduism, which may help in her research. Internally, Shruti hoped this excursion would bring Ramesh and Dr. Markesic closer. Aryan was quietly smiling, looking at the wits of his beloved wife. Aryan, Shruti, her mother, and little Rishi returned home from the orphanage.

Ramesh and Dr. Markesic embraced Shruti's idea and explored the temple. While they visited the exquisitely crafted Swaminarayan Mandir together, they were secretly thrilled by Shruti's thoughtful planning. After spending some time in the temple's serene surroundings, they strolled through its beautiful gardens, relished a light and music show in the evening, and shared dinner before concluding the delightful evening. Through this encounter, they felt they had known each other for years.

In the following days, Dr. Markesic had limited interaction with the couple. She had to participate in a gynecological doctors' conference and present her research paper on the psychological aspects of maternal influence on fetal development. Her colleagues and doctors appreciated her innovative work, which she hoped would benefit many prospective parents. She wanted to identify a suitable match to experience such a divine blessing on herself. Being a young doctor of thirty years, she was looking for a like-minded life partner and became increasingly dreaming of a holy soul to incarnate as her child. Ramesh was in her mind, but it was too early and required much more thinking. Despite her busy schedule involving working with the most reputed Dr. Shweta at her nursing home, occasional university visits, and weekly visits to Aryan and Shruti, she found solace in participating in weekly meditation sessions.

-x-

Chapter 3: Align Polestar to Cosmos

Picture courtesy: https://thecosmostree.com

Finance Polestar and Goddess Lakshmi

Strategy Polestar and Lord Ganesha

HR Polestar and Bhagwan Rama

Quality Polestar and Lord Vishwakarma

Marketing Polestar and Indra Deva

Engineering Polestar and Goddess Sarasvati

Technology Polestar and Agni Deva

Supply Chain Polestar and Varuna Deva

Empower Limitless Vision

Finance Polestar and Goddess Lakshmi

"Let us meditate on the Great Goddess Sri Lakshmi, the consort of Sri Maha Vishnu, and may her inspiration and illumination enlighten our minds."
- Shri Lakshmi Gayatri Mantra.

There was no post- group mediation interactive session for the next two Saturdays. Neither Ramesh nor Dr. Markesic could come even for group meditation. On the following Saturday, as they gathered after the group meditation, both Ramesh and Dr. Markesic appeared content, suggesting they had fully enjoyed their visit to the temple and each other's company. Jokingly, Shruti smiled and asked Dr. Markesic about her experience during the temple visit. Dr. Markesic grinned, "We had a wonderful time together, and we thanked Shruti for giving this wonderful idea." Ramesh delightfully added they had some delightful moments together, followed by dinner after the temple visit.

To change the topic of conversation, Dr. Markesic turned to Aryan and inquired about developing functional polestars. Aryan explained that it was an inspirational journey. To attain something significant in life, our polestar, or a big dream, motivates us to explore further. Dr. Markesic agreed that this research project encouraged her to learn how they could teach specific values to little Rishi.

Aryan added that the company's vision might be cascaded to the department level as a functional polestar to motivate the employees to align themselves with their big dream to attain excellence. Excellence in work creates a win-win situation. When an employee excels, he grows in his career, and the company attains perfection, customer delight, and a learning environment. On the initiative of the

Empower Limitless Vision

Finance Head, his company planned to organize the Finance function workshop to evolve Finance Polestar.

Robin made logistic arrangements for the full-day workshop with help from Sophia. Finance Head Thomas requested CEO John to preside over the workshop. The top management team, alongside all Finance Section Heads and their enthusiastic team members, totaling about 35 individuals, participated in the workshop.

Two days before the workshop, Aryan shared his ideas with Finance Head Thomas about associating the Finance Polestar with Goddess Lakshmi, the Goddess of Wealth and Prosperity. Thomas felt inspired and wanted to incorporate Goddess Lakshmi's virtues into the Finance Polestar. Thomas, a strong admirer of Aryan, suggested that Aryan share his thoughts at the beginning of the workshop. He believed it would set the tone for developing the functional Polestars of other departments and pave the way for devising some innovative parameters. Aryan readily agreed to this proposal.

As the host department head, Thomas warmly welcomed all the workshop participants. He outlined the significant responsibilities of the Finance function, which included managing expenses, revenue, and cash flow, budgeting, cost control, financial forecasting, financial reporting and analysis, tax planning and compliances, and capital expenditure planning. After briefly explaining these responsibilities, Thomas invited CEO John to inaugurate the workshop formally.

During his speech, John stressed the importance of the Functional Polestar in driving excellence across the function. He praised Thomas for taking the lead and emphasized that a company's success depends on its financial performance. He said the main objective of the finance function is **"to ensure positive and increasing**

Empower Limitless Vision

trend in Economic Value Addition (EVA) through the effectiveness of Finance process." John asked Aryan to share his Hindu mythological perspective of correlating Goddess Lakshmi with the finance function.

Goddess Lakshmi and Finance Function

Aryan began by reciting the **Shri Lakshmi Gayatri Mantra**, invoking the blessings of Goddess Lakshmi - the Hindu deity associated with wealth, prosperity, abundance, and financial insight. The chanting of this mantra promotes a positive flow of money and attracts wealth, fostering success. The Finance function focuses on the strategic goals and objectives, encompassing the following key elements:

1. Finance entails the management of money, investments, and resources to foster wealth creation and economic growth, aligning with Lakshmi's association with wealth.

2. Lakshmi symbolizes material and spiritual prosperity, mirroring Finance's aspiration for financial stability, growth, and abundance.

3. The lotus held by Lakshmi signifies the smooth adoption of ethical practices and strong governance, ensuring financial stability.

4. Lakshmi's association with good fortune success inspires the finance function to exhibit agility, innovation, and adaptability to change, utilize technology for a quick transition, drive financial success, and make profitable investments.

5. Finance acts as a strategic partner, offering insights, analysis, and guidance for decision-making, fostering growth, and forging alliances internally with strategic planning and externally with banks, like the

collaboration between Goddess Lakshmi and Lord Ganesha during "Lakshmi Pujan."

6. *Being "Chanchala," Lakshmi frequently changes hands and quickly moves from one to another, representing "Flow." Similarly, the Finance function should ensure a consistent flow of funds through effective risk management, timely payments to creditors, and prudent debtor management.*

Quoting CEO John Aryan added that inspired by Goddess Lakshmi, the Finance function should focus on positively driving Economic Value Addition (EVA) by optimizing finance processes. It requires fostering a culture of collective financial responsibility by empowering the employees to take ethical financial decisions and thus ensure honest wealth creation.

Aryan clarified that the comparison between the Finance department and Goddess Lakshmi is symbolic. Still, it underscores the principles of wealth management, prosperity, and success that hold significance for individuals and organizations. His analogy received broad appreciation from the participants. It is followed by brainstorming.

Finance Polestar and its Parameters

The group agreed that Economic Value Added (EVA) is a reliable metric for evaluating a company's financial performance. Thomas explained that the robustness and immunity of EVA from fraudulent accounting practices have led to its widespread adoption by numerous American companies. Stewart & Co. introduced EVA in the late 1980s, a more accurate measure of financial performance than traditional metrics such as earnings per share or return on investment. EVA deducts the cost of capital from operating profit, offering a genuine measure of economic gain and factoring in future investments for forward-looking analysis. It aligns management incentives with shareholder interests, promotes long-term value creation, and enables performance comparisons across various companies. They evolved the following Finance Polestar:

"To optimize finance processes, cash-flow and growth in Economic Value Addition (EVA), nurture a culture of honesty and shared financial responsibility in decision-making."

A participant suggested using the word "vision" instead of the term "Finance Polestar." John appreciated his idea and said Polestar is a celestial body that remains fixed in the night sky and has been a reference point for ages. To retrieve our commitment to drawing wisdom from ancient traditions, the term "Polestar" has been chosen to symbolize this dedication. Everyone agreed on it.

John commended Thomas and Aryan. He suggested setting measurable parameters and annual targets to assess progress toward achieving the Finance Polestar. In the post-lunch session, John and most top management team members departed, leaving Thomas to preside over the meeting. They finalized the following measurement parameters and targets:

1. **EVA growth rate:** A Target of a 5% increase over the previous year was set, with an aspirational goal of achieving 10% growth.

2. **Return on Investment (ROI):** ROI reflects the efficacy of financial decisions and measures the return generated by investments relative to the cost of capital. The target for ROI was to surpass the Cost of Capital.

3. **Cost of capital:** Factors like the company's financing structure, industry, and location contribute to the cost

Empower Limitless Vision

of capital. The target was to keep it below the industry average.

4. **Employee financial literacy:** To continually measure employees' financial skills and ensure 80% of finance employees possess basic financial literacy. It helps in building a culture of shared financial responsibility.

5. **Honest and Shared Financial Decisions:** This parameter is essential for providing appropriate training and guidance to employees in making informed, shared, and fair financial decisions. The target was to ensure that 100% of decisions were honest.

Ultimately, Thomas emphasized that these objectives serve as guiding parameters to achieve the Finance function's Polestar. Additionally, they will continue to work on routine financial metrics like Net Profit Margin, Gross Profit Margin, Revenue Growth, Debt-to-Equity Ratio, and Operating Expense Ratio, as previously monitored.

A CFA and financial consultant, Ramesh appreciated Aryan's innovative approach and said, "Wow! You are charting a new direction for managing the Finance function." Dr. Markesic had little interest in mathematics and was weak in managing finances. She felt happy that Ramesh had endorsed the Aryan's approach to evolving the Finance Polestar. The inclusion of the phrase 'honesty and shared financial responsibility in decision making' in the Polestar fascinated her. Suddenly, little Rishi, nestled in his grandmother's lap, burst into laughter, bringing smiles to the faces of everyone in the room. With this, they closed the Saturday post-meditation session for the day.

Strategy Polestar and Lord Ganesha

OM, let us meditate upon the one-tusked (or one-toothed) God. May the curved-trunked one inspire and illuminate us. May he guide our intellect and wisdom.

- Ganesha Gayatri Mantra

The following Saturday, at the beginning of the post-meditation meeting, Dr. Markesic asked Aryan to share his next steps. *Aryan replied that the Goddess Lakshmi stays with Lord Ganesha, the 'Prathama Pujya' or the first deity to be worshipped.* He felt that the next functional Polestar should be related to Ganesha. Dr. Markesic was fascinated by it because she had seen the statue of Ganesha during her maiden visit to the Swaminarayan temple with Ramesh.

The Ganesha Story

Dr. Markesic asked why Ganesha has an iconic elephant-headed form. Aryan replied that a few Hindu mythological stories are associated with Ganesha's birth and elephant head. These stories vary in narration in different regions of India based on local traditions and culture. He shared the story that his grandfather had narrated to him during childhood. Everyone was keen to listen to the story. Shruti's mother added that we usually live in a joint family in India, but as the children moved to other places due to their jobs, the family tradition weakened. As a result, the children miss learning the traditional values from their grandparents.

Aryan said the goddess Parvati was lonely and longed for affection. Her consort, the Hindu god of destruction, God Shiva, was meditating on Mount Kailash. She collected the turmeric paste (for bathing) and sweat from her body, molded it into a statue of a young boy, and

Empower Limitless Vision

breathed life into it through her divine powers. Thus, Parvati's son Ganesha was born.

One day, Parvati went to bathe, asking her son to stand as a guard outside her chamber. Meanwhile, Shiva returned from Mount Kailash and was prevented from entering his own house by the young boy following his mother's orders! Furious, Shiva was unaware of the boy and ordered his divine attendants (Ganas) to destroy him. Despite their best efforts, they could not defeat the young boy, who possessed the combined strength of Parvati and the divine dirt used to create him.

Realizing the extraordinary powers of this boy, the other gods, including Lord Brahma and Lord Vishnu, intervened to stop the battle. However, the usually peaceful Shiva, using His divine fury, severed Ganesha's head, killing him instantly.

When Parvati learned of this, She was so enraged and insulted that She decided to destroy the entire Creation! Lord Brahma, Lord Vishnu, and all other deities pleaded that She reconsider Her decision. She agreed to review to see if her two conditions were fulfilled. First, Ganesha would be brought back to life, and second, he would be worshipped before all other deities.

Lord Shiva agreed to Parvati's conditions to console Her, who was devastated by the loss of her son. He asked Lord Brahma to go and bring the head of the first creature he crossed with its head facing North. Brahma soon returned with the head of a strong elephant, which Shiva placed onto Ganesha's body. Breathing new life into him, Shiva declared Ganesha to be His son, gave him the status of the leader of all Ganas, and named him Ganapati. Subsequently, Lord Brahma, Vishnu, and all other deities blessed Ganesha with their divine powers. Lord Shiva

Empower Limitless Vision

decreed that Ganesha would always be worshipped first in any ritual.

Ganesha's unwavering devotion to his mother, his role as a protector, and his unique appearance made him a beloved and highly revered deity for removing obstacles and ensuring the success of new beginnings. Ganesha is also the patron saint of the arts. Dr. Markesic was satisfied and asked Aryan to continue with Strategy Polestar formulation.

Aryan said that since Ganesha is worshiped first amongst all deities and relates to strategic planning, he requested that John keep the next session to evolve the Functional Polestar of Strategic Planning. Further, Strategy Polestar and its parameters would help spread wisdom and ensure holistic planning by all functions. Considering that the exercise had to be quickly completed for all departments, CEO John agreed to his proposal.

Strategy Polestar and Measurable Parameters

Hanna, the planning coordinator, organized the logistics and invited key participants, including CEO John, the head of strategic planning. All Functional Heads and Coordinators gathered, expecting valuable insights.

CEO John, inspired by his discussion with Aryan, commenced the session by emphasizing Lord Ganesha's significance as the deity associated with unlimited wisdom and planning. He stressed that meticulous planning overcomes the execution challenges and helps to attain excellence in life. He outlined the following roles of Strategic Planning:

a) *Formulating strategic and long-term plans, monitoring annual plans, and devising efficient management systems.*
b) *Catalyzing organizational excellence in all aspects of organizational processes.*

Empower Limitless Vision

c) *Driving innovative improvement initiatives to ensure increased employee engagement and motivation levels.*
d) *Updating Capital Assets to maintain competitiveness.*

John explained that invoking Lord Ganesha represents a wise approach to conducting financial, quality, environmental, and social audits /assessments. It helps in evolving strategies for making improvements to attain sustainable success. While participants appreciated John's insights, John asked Aryan to lead the discussion further.

Reciting the Ganesha Gayatri Mantra, Aryan underscored its transformative influence, enabling surmounting obstacles, acquiring wisdom, and achieving success. Stressing Ganesha's pivotal role in strategic planning, he highlighted the deity's contributions to clarity, foresight, and a holistic perspective. In monitoring plans, Aryan linked Ganesha's attributes to anticipating challenges, discovering innovative solutions, and cultivating efficient management systems.

Lord Ganesha, offspring of Lord Shiva and Goddess Parvati, holds a revered position in the Trinity and is invoked at the outset of rituals for obstacle removal and ensuring success. Aryan emphasized the necessity of in-depth planning to commence significant tasks, be it a new project development, a new task, an examination, or any other endeavor.

As the God of Wisdom, Ganesha's large elephant head symbolizes profound knowledge. Worshiping Ganesha aligns with clarity of thought, intelligence, and the capacity to make astute decisions, embodying research, foresight, and a holistic approach to strategic planning.

Aryan metaphorically associated Ganesha's intelligence and resourcefulness with developing efficient management systems. He inspired planners to create seamless processes, allocate ample resources, and optimize operations. Invoking Ganesha's blessings symbolizes gathering your wisdom in decision-making and ensuring a successful and auspicious outcome in planning and execution. Subsequently, thorough discussions led to the emergence of the following functional Polestar for Strategic Planning:

"Inspired by Lord Ganesha's wisdom, to excel in strategic planning, fostering organizational excellence through innovative initiatives, efficient systems, and a commitment to continual growth."

The group finalized the following parameters and annual targets:

1. **Strategic Plan Alignment:** Ensure 80% alignment between strategic plan objectives and annual organizational/ functional goals. Conduct monthly monitoring and reviews.

2. **Strategic Plan Adoption Rate:** To ensure 90% of employees actively use and implement the strategic plan during the year.

3. **Innovation Index:** To implement at least three company-level innovative projects that contribute to growth.

4. **Reduction in Operational Costs**: Achieve 8% cost reduction in all areas of operation over the previous year.

5. **Cycle Time Reduction:** Achieve a 15% reduction in end-to-end process cycle time in all areas.

6. **Employee Engagement Index**: Conduct surveys to assess employee engagement and draw action plans to sustain employee engagement above 80%.

Empower Limitless Vision

7. **Growth in Capital Assets:** Achieve a 5% growth in the value of updated capital assets.

8. **Customer satisfaction:** Conduct customer surveys annually and draw action plans to maintain customer satisfaction levels above 90%.

9. **Cost of Innovation:** Reduce the cost per successful innovation initiative by 10% compared to the previous year.

10. **Use data and analytics:** Utilize data and analytics for informed decision-making, trend analysis, demand forecasting, and improvement opportunities.

11. **Monitor and evaluate performance:** Establish key performance indicators (KPIs) to measure periodic outcomes, identify areas for improvement, and take corrective measures as required.

Dr. Markesic, Ramesh, and others marveled at the remarkable evolution of the functional Polestar and its parameters. It looked like a guide for aspiring companies to follow.

As lunchtime approached, Shruti graciously invited everyone for lunch. Internally, a sense of humility lingered amongst all participants. Week after week, they attended group meditation led by Aryan, who shared his experiences of nurturing little Rishi before his birth. Shruti and her mother extended their unbroken love and care besides their profound hospitality. Aryan and Shruti, driven by a deep respect for the Himalayan Sadhu and his boundless love and teachings, felt happy to be the hosts. The Sadhu, a spiritual powerhouse, effortlessly discerned their thoughts and swiftly arranged every comfort using his divine powers.

Post-lunch, the participants departed, carrying a mental commitment to return the following Saturday, honoring the ongoing connection forged in the embrace of Aryan and Shruti's hospitality and the profound teachings of the Himalayan Sadhu. Rishi's third monthly milestone birthday was coming on Wednesday, 28th June. Aryan and Shruti made the necessary arrangements and purchased the gifts for the children on Sunday for distribution at the orphanage. Subsequently, they visited the orphanage on Wednesday and happily celebrated Rishi's birthday.

-x-

HR Polestar and Bhagwan Rama

We meditate upon Lord Narayana, who is known as Vasudeva. May Lord Vishnu enlighten our intellect and inspire us.
- Shri Vishnu Gayatri Mantra

On the ensuing Saturday, after the group meditation session, Dr. Markesic initiated a discussion. She requested Aryan to share his insights on Bhagwan Rama, expressing a desire to deepen her understanding after encountering Rama in her readings and social media. Aryan agreed to her request.

Story of Bhagwan Rama

Aryan delved into Hindu mythology, explaining the Trinity: Brahma, Vishnu, and Shiva having unique roles in steering the universe. Brahma, the creator, embodies the genesis of all existence, while Vishnu, the preserver, sustains the cosmic order and harmony. Shiva, the destroyer and regenerator, signifies the transformative forces in the eternal cycle of creation and dissolution. These are their symbiotic roles in forming the cosmic equilibrium, guiding the celestial realms, and influencing the fabric of existence in Hindu cosmology.

Lord Vishnu, the preserver, incarnated time and again in various forms, known as avatars, to restore cosmic order and protect dharma (righteousness). The ten avatars of Lord Vishnu are Matsya (The Fish), Kurma (The Tortoise), Varaha (The Boar), Narasimha (The Man-Lion), Vamana (The Dwarf), Parashurama, Rama, Krishna, Buddha, and Kalki. Each avatar of Lord Vishnu symbolizes a unique aspect of cosmic harmony, divine intervention, and the eternal struggle between good and evil.

Empower Limitless Vision

The seventh avatar of Vishnu incarnated as Lord Rama to defeat the demon king Ravana, who had become a threat to the cosmic order. Rama's life, teachings, and actions hold profound spiritual and moral significance, emphasizing the eternal principles of righteousness and the ultimate victory of dharma over adharma. His story, narrated in the epic Ramayana, inspires millions on their spiritual journeys and emphasizes the triumph of virtue over vice. It also serves as a leadership model for the corporate world.

Aryan said that Rama is the most popular Hindu deity irrespective of caste, creed, religion, or geography. Various versions of his life history exist globally, but the story narrated in the epic Valmiki Ramayana is deemed the most authentic.

Bhagwan Rama was born to King Dasharatha of Ayodhya and Queen Kaushalya during Treta Yuga (A defined period in the cosmic cycle). His childhood and early life exhibit exemplary virtues, notably his unwavering devotion to dharma (righteousness). Rishi Vishwamitra sought King Dasharatha's permission to take Rama and his younger brother Lakshmana to protect Sadhus and Saints, perform Yajna, and live in the forests, shielding them from demonic torment. Rama and Lakshmana valiantly vanquished demons led by Khar and Dushan. Rama won the bow competition set by king Janaka of Mithila and married his daughter Sita. His brothers Lakshmana, Bharata, and Shatrughna also entered marital unions.

As preparations unfolded to declare Rama as the king of Ayodhya, queen Kaikeyi, influenced by her maid Manthara, demanded Rama's exile for fourteen years and the coronation of her son Bharata. Rama accepted this willingly and left for the forest accompanied by his wife Sita and loyal brother Lakshmana. King Dasharatha could not tolerate this painful decision and expired. Despite Bharata's efforts to persuade Rama to return, he insisted on fulfilling his father's promise. It signifies Rama's attainment of a Sthitaprajya Samadhi of unwavering wisdom and steady consciousness.

The narrative unfolded further with the abduction of Sita by the demon king Ravana in Rama's absence. A quest to find Sita ensued, led by Rama, aided by the monkey-God Hanuman and an army of monkeys under Sugriva. The construction of the Ram Setu (bridge to Lanka) and the subsequent fierce battle culminated in Rama's victory over Ravana, rescuing Sita. Sita underwent a trial by fire (Agnipariksha) to prove her purity. The remains of Ram Setu in the sea near Rameswaram in India are one of the testimonies of the epic thousands of years ago.

After completing the exile, Rama returned to Ayodhya with Sita and Lakshmana, where Bharata and all the citizens joyously welcomed them. Rama was crowned king and his kingdom prospered. Ram-Rajya (Kingdom of Rama) is the symbol of prosperity and righteousness.

Aryan concluded that the Ramayana is not just a mythological account but also imparts moral and ethical lessons through the life of Lord Rama.

Dr. Markesic was deeply captivated by Rama's story and found great inspiration in its magnificence. The discussion continued, involving other participants, with Ramesh posing a question about the corporate function to which Bhagwan Rama could be related. They felt that Rama might be correlated with HR function and asked Aryan to continue the story for the evolution of HR Polestar.

Evolution of HR Polestar

CEO John's appreciation for Finance and Strategic Planning functions instigated a sense of urgency among other functions. Aryan, the most sought-after facilitator, turned his attention to HR at the request of HR Head Victor. Victor wanted the HR Polestar finalization before the upcoming performance appraisal cycle in March. Emma, the HR coordinator, organized the workshop logistics, inviting all coordinators, section heads, and a few bright mid-level HR executives. Victor emphasized HR as a collective responsibility, invited all Functional Heads, and requested CEO John to chair the meeting.

On 24 February 2023, Victor welcomed all participants in the full-day meeting and shared an overview of HR activities like recruitment, employee onboarding and offboarding, compensation and benefits administration, employee relations and wellbeing, training and development, and compliance with labor laws. Additionally, HR was responsible for all regulatory, environmental, and legal compliances, contracts, litigation, intellectual property, etc. Victor then invited John to inaugurate the meeting.

CEO John underscored the significance of HR in individual lives and organizational purpose, aligning it with the well-being of humankind. He said **HR enhances value to employees & society, resulting in a committed and highly motivated workforce for the achievement of business objectives & striving for a better quality of life for the community.** It also builds a better work environment and enhances employee engagement. He invited Aryan to share his HR perspective, linked to Hindu mythology.

Aryan chanting the Shri Vishnu Gayatri Mantra sought Lord Vishnu's blessings for HR professionals. He said everyone has looked for Rama-Rajya for thousands of years as it provided happiness and prosperity to all. The role of HR is to materialize this dream of the employees. Lord Rama, the 7th avatar of Lord Vishnu, is ideal for HR professionals. Rama's qualities emphasize maintaining the vital balance between emotions and conduct. Rama is also known as Maryada Puroshotama. His benevolence, compassion, and commitment to righteousness resonated with HR's aim to establish fairness and harmony between the organization and its employees. By cultivating an environment rooted in kindness and justice, HR professionals can create a supportive and inclusive space where every employee feels valued, respected, and treated fairly.

By creating a positive and ethical work culture, HR professionals actively contribute to the overall well-being and success of the organization. Employees seek enlightenment, intellectual growth, and inspiration from Rama, recognizing these as essential for effective HR leadership. Meditating on Him enables HR leaders to cultivate more profound compassion, crucial for nurturing growth, success, and humility. Moreover, Rama's energy and power advocate for collaboration, aligning the HR function towards fostering diversity, inclusivity, and innovation across various HR roles, such as recruitment, promotion, and training.

Aryan's narrative on the role of HR and its alignment with Bhagwan Rama left a lasting impression on everyone present. Following detailed discussions, the HR Polestar was crystallized as follows:

Empower Limitless Vision

"To foster a dynamic, diverse, and ethical workforce dedicated to excellence through learning, innovation, collaboration, and communication. We strive to improve employee well-being and enhance the quality of life in society."

To conclude, John highlighted the parallel between Bhagwan Rama's principles of preservation and HR's role in maintaining balance and harmony. Embodying these qualities, HR professionals can create a nurturing work environment, contributing to organizational success. John entrusted HR Head Victor with evolving measurable parameters and targets based on the HR Polestar.

In the post-lunch session, Victor chaired the meeting as the CEO, and a few Functional Heads left to address some urgent matters of respective domains. The group identified measurable parameters and annual targets for the HR Polestar, covering diversity and inclusion, ethical conduct, talent management, learning culture, employee-driven innovations, performance management, collaboration, communication, employee engagement, and work-life balance as detailed below:

1. **Diversity and inclusion**: The workforce diversity ratio should reflect broader population demographics at various locations. Reduce the diversity gap by 5% during the year.

2. **Compliance and ethical standards**: To ensure that all HR policies and practices 100% comply with legal and ethical standards.

3. **Talent management and succession planning**: Identify 20% of employees as high potential through a 360-degree evaluation and groom them to acquire 80% of leadership positions.

Empower Limitless Vision

4. **Learning culture**: To ensure at least 80% of employees participate in annual training programs and achieve an average 40-hour training per employee.

5. **Employee-driven Innovations**: To implement at least three kaizens/ suggestions per employee annually.

6. **Performance management effectiveness**: Ensure 90% completion of the individual /group annual performance targets that align with the company's strategic objectives.

7. **Collaboration**: Every employee must participate in at least two cross-functional teams annually.

8. **Communication**: To ensure a 5% increase in employees reporting 'high satisfaction' in employee surveys on internal communication parameters.

9. **Employee engagement**: Achieve a minimum score of 80% in employee engagement surveys.

10. **Work-life balance**: Achieve an 80% satisfaction score on the work-life balance parameter in employee surveys through flexible working hours, working from home, etc.

11. **Quality of life for society**: Spend 2% of profit before tax on corporate social responsibility during the year. Besides, undertake two environmental sustainability initiatives annually and encourage employees to volunteer for community outreach initiatives.

Quality Head Felix commended the HR function for their exhaustive exercise. He invited all functional heads to participate in the Quality function's meeting on Tuesday. Victor concluded the meeting by thanking everyone and urging active involvement to achieve the set parameters. He

Empower Limitless Vision

emphasized that HR is a custodian, enabler, and facilitator of HR processes, requiring collaboration from all leaders.

-x-

Quality Polestar and Lord Vishwakarma

"You alone are Vishwakarma, the creator of all works. You alone are the craftsman of the entire universe. You alone are Vishnu, the Supreme Lord, and Hari. You alone manifest all that is auspicious."
— Prayer to Lord Vishwakarma.

Next Saturday, Dr. Markesic, Ramesh, and other participants of the post-group meditation interaction were keen to know what happened after the evolution of HR Polestar. The discussion begins with Dr. Markesic's remarks. She said that during March 2023, Shruti was already in the ninth month of pregnancy. Luckily, she did not face any significant gyne issues as encountered by many would-be mothers. Shruti praised Dr. Shweta, Markesic, and her family for taking utmost care of her during this critical period. She also attributed it to divine bliss.

Aryan said his deadline for completing the evolution of the Polestar exercise was mid-March, as year-end pressure was increasing in the office and a few functions were still left. Also, he had to take care of Shruti. Besides, her healthy mindset and wellness were essential to learning the concept and actively contributing, which may help Rishi learn many more thoughts in prenatal conditions. Little Rishi was spreading a mysterious smile in his grandmother's lap. Aryan said that he would be narrating the evolution of Quality function today.

Following the evolution of three functional Polestars, Felix, the Quality Head, felt a moral imperative to conclude the Quality Polestar swiftly. As the sole remaining member of the Apex Thinktank responsible for driving excellence, his area was lagging. Felix had already

Empower Limitless Vision

announced Tuesday as the meeting date and invited all Functional Heads. He pursued Aryan and Quality Coordinator Sophia to organize a full-day meeting to develop the Quality Polestar and its measurable parameters. Recognizing the significant support from Sophia and Felix in driving the excellence initiatives, Aryan fully assisted Sophia in extending invitations to all Quality section heads, selecting subordinates with a positive outlook, and arranging the logistics for the meeting. Felix requested John to preside over the inaugural session.

At the onset of the meeting, Felix delineated the responsibilities and tasks of the quality function, encompassing aspects such as implementing quality control standards, inspecting and testing products and services for defects, and initiating quality improvements. Additionally, he highlighted the Quality department's support to other departments in manufacturing and processing, setting production schedules, ensuring consistent quality products and services, inventory control, maintenance of facilities and equipment, and providing a safe working environment.

Felix then invited John to commence the meeting with insightful remarks. John underscored the pivotal role of quality in individual lives and organizational excellence. He emphasized that quality is not a cost but a necessity; neglecting it can result in significant consequences. Failing quality jeopardizes corporate sustainability and leads to a path of failure. John interconnected quality with the company's work culture and values, stressing the responsibility of each individual. He expected every person to execute their duties with 100% accuracy, highlighting that even if ten employees consecutively achieved 99% accuracy, the overall quality level would drop to 90%, an unacceptable standard for customers.

John concluded that **the quality function should focus on building quality into the product through**

'Defect prevention' and providing prompt and efficient quality services. He asked Aryan to share his mythological perspective on quality. Everyone was keen to listen to yet another unique mythological perspective from Aryan.

Ramesh quipped that it means your colleagues were also as keen to listen to your mythological stories as we all are listening to now. Aryan smiled, nodded his head in affirmation, and continued.

Aryan began by reciting a mantra dedicated to invoking Lord Vishwakarma with a prayer: *"To all the works done here and there, O Lord of the Universe, Salutations, salutations to Lord Vishwakarma."*

Before Aryan could proceed further, Dr. Markesic asked Aryan to share the story of Lord Vishwakarma.

Story of Lord Vishwakarma

Aryan portrayed Lord Vishwakarma as the divine architect, master craftsman, and ultimate creator in Hindu mythology. In the cosmic dawn, Lord Vishwakarma emerged from the cosmic loom. His eyes held the secrets of creation, and his fingers danced across the warp and weft of existence. He shaped the cosmos with expertise that transcends time, molding delicate lotus petals and crafting grand arches for celestial palaces. *Aryan emphasized the diverse facets of Lord Vishwakarma, recognizing him as the divine architect, master craftsman, and ultimate creator. Vishwakarma created the galaxies, planets, and constellations. He created suns to illuminate the darkness and the moon in the night sky—a beacon for lovers and dreamers.* He sculpted marvels like the majestic Himalayas on Earth and built the celestial city of Swarga, where gods and goddesses dwelled in palaces adorned with cosmic art.

Empower Limitless Vision

Despite his divine stature, Vishwakarma faced challenges and quality issues. With patience and wisdom, he unraveled cosmic knots, maintaining the fabric of time and ensuring cosmic balance. Vishwakarma's legacy lives on in hymns of artisans, architects, and engineers. Vishwakarma is the source of all auspiciousness as the weaver of worlds and the inspiration behind human ingenuity. Aryan concluded that invoking his blessings, guidance, and protection is essential for success in both professional and creative pursuits. Then, he proceeded to narrate how Quality Polestar evolved.

Evolution of Quality Polestar

Aryan then connected the evolution of quality with the symbolic association of Lord Vishwakarma. He emphasized quality as a fundamental aspect of any product or service, aligning with Vishwakarma's role in planning and design. Drawing parallels, Aryan linked Vishwakarma's dedication to perfection, continuous learning, innovation, and problem-solving with various aspects of quality management.

Lord Vishwakarma's association with architecture underscores structural integrity and design aesthetics, which are essential in various industries. His skilled craftsmanship reflects the precision required in quality control, ensuring meticulous attention to detail in crafting products or services. As a symbol of continuous learning and improvement, Vishwakarma aligns with Quality Management principles, emphasizing constant improvement, meeting customer expectations, and fostering innovation. His role in overcoming challenges parallels the problem-solving aspect of quality assurance. Vishwakarma's commitment to excellence in craftsmanship symbolizes the overarching dedication to quality that organizations strive for. Establishing a quality culture within the organization aligns with his pursuit of creating perfect and flawless creations, reflecting a commitment to high standards and continuous enhancement in the quality function.

He concluded that the symbolic comparison highlights principles such as excellence, attention to detail, continuous improvement, total commitment, and passion for achieving and maintaining high-quality standards. Quality professionals and leaders draw inspiration from these divine qualities of Vishwakarma.

The meeting delved into an extensive discussion on the Quality vision for nearly three hours. The group unanimously agreed on a robust defect prevention system that is compliant with regulatory requirements and supportive of ethical decision-making to enhance the company's efficiency and effectiveness. The consensus was that Quality drives a culture of excellence and customer delight, ensuring products and services meet ethical standards and provide value to customers and stakeholders. Based on the deliberations, the group finalized the Quality Polestar statement:

"Foster a culture of excellence to deliver effective services for customer success and value enhancement to stakeholders by continually seeking knowledge, learning new techniques, improving processes, and preventing defects."

In the post-lunch session, the group identified the following measurable parameters and annual targets to realize the Quality Polestar and ensure its effective implementation:

1. **<u>Customer Satisfaction</u>**: Achieve a minimum customer satisfaction score of 90% and ensure an increase of 5% in delighted customers.

2. **Compliance**: Ensure 100% compliance with laid norms for all processes, products, and services annually.

3. **Defect Rate**: To measure the defect rate to reduce it to below 1%.

4. **Process efficiency**: Improve process efficiency by 5% annually and maintain it above 85%.

5. **Quality-related Training**: Ensure 100% of employees participate in quality-related training and increase training hours per employee by 10%.

6. **Cost of Quality**: Reducing cost of quality (total cost of preventing, detecting, and correcting quality issues) by 5%.

7. **Continual Improvement:** Involving 10% more employees Y-o-Y in quality improvement initiatives.

8. **Ethical Performance Index**: Maintaining an ethical performance index of 90% or higher.

9. **Supplier Quality**: Increasing the percentage of products or services from suppliers that meet quality standards by 5% annually.

10. **First Pass Yield:** To achieve 95% or higher first pass yield.

11. **Time to Resolve Quality Issues**: Resolving 95% of quality issues within a specific timeframe.

In conclusion, Felix thanked all Heads and requested that they encourage active involvement from all employees in building a culture of excellence in the company.

Following Aryan's conclusion of his narration, Dr. Markesic and others posed a few questions to seek clarification, bringing the day's session to a close. However, even after the session ended, usually cheerful Sophia sat with a gloomy face. Shruti inquired about her sadness, to which Sophia responded, "You know very well."

Aryan's imminent departure from the company next week, on Friday, July 14, 2023, after six years, was upsetting her. The news of Aryan's resignation became public the day before after the quarterly review of the results. The sudden development took everyone aback, while Aryan and Shruti were smiling. Shruti revealed that Aryan had resigned three months ago but kept it a secret following management's request. While accepting his resignation with a heavy heart, CEO John requested Aryan to stay until the review of the first quarterly results, to which Aryan agreed. Aryan calmly added that they were not going elsewhere; instead, he would launch his startup very soon. The conversation concluded swiftly as they had to complete the packing and last-minute purchases for Shruti's mother's return to India on Sunday after spending about six months with them.

-x-

Marketing Polestar and Indra Deva

"Swift, firm, mighty, not terrifying, dense like a thundercloud, shaking the strong foundations. With an unwinking and one-pointed glance, Indra, with a hundred hosts, won the battle."
- Rigveda - 10/103/1

The return of Shruti's mother back to India brought a void in their life. As the days swiftly elapsed, the Friday, July 14th, appeared, marking the moment to bid farewell to Aryan. He had resigned from a prosperous job and a commendable association of colleagues, paving the way for a brighter future. Aryan's departure posed challenges for both admirers and critics alike. The Young Thinktank organized a grand farewell for Aryan's departure, with Shruti and little Rishi being the Guest of Honour. Many employees gathered to bid farewell and express their gratitude towards Aryan. His meditation sessions and knowledge of Hindu mythology have made a special place in everyone's heart. His ability to link corporate working with ancient wisdom impressed them. Despite grooming Sophia to carry forward his responsibilities, the void left by Aryan remained unfilled at the senior level despite numerous attempts to find a suitable replacement. CEO John announced that as soon as Aryan opens his consultancy Startup, they will sign a Consultancy Agreement with his Startup. Everyone appreciated this gesture and gave Sophia some consolation.

The following day, after the group meditation, participants learned about Aryan's resignation. They discussed Aryan's future course of action and pledged their full support for the venture. Aryan and Shruti, calm and composed, adapted to the significant change in their lives, surprising others. Aryan had already begun focused preparations for his startup, while Shruti felt a void with her mother's return to India. The stage was meticulously set for a new beginning and an entrepreneurial venture.

After everyone left, they commenced the post-meditation discussion session, which was delayed by almost an hour. Dr. Markesic, Sophia, Nancy, and Ramesh participated. Nancy cared for little Rishi, a role previously handled by Shruti's mother.

Replying to Dr. Markesic's queries regarding developing the next functional polestar, Aryan redirected his energies to revitalizing memories related to the Marketing Polestar.

He began his narration by stating that with half of the corporate functions' Polestars finalized, coordinators and heads, including James from Marketing, urgently sought to complete the exercise. They requested Aryan's assistance to complete the process by mid-March. CEO John pushed the activity to synchronize target setting with the Balanced Scorecard for the next fiscal year. The excellence journey gained momentum, with various functions becoming more proactive. Some employees had undertaken individual improvement projects. Aryan's reputation at the company soared due to his unique skills, knowledge, and virtues, turning former foes into fans.

The Marketing Head asked Aryan and Marketing Coordinator James to organize the full-day meeting for the function on Friday, 3rd March 23. CEO John agreed to chair it. All logistic arrangements were in place, as the people concerned understood the requirements in the previous four workshops.

Welcoming the participants in the workshop, the Marketing Head outlined his department's broad role and responsibilities. He said the department covers sales, marketing, and customer service functions. These included market research, target identification, strategy development, advertising, digital marketing, customer relationship management, quota achievement, issue resolution, and maintaining customer satisfaction through feedback analysis. The workshop showcased the multifaceted nature of the Marketing department's roles and emphasized the skills required for success in the dynamic business landscape. He invited CEO John to inaugurate the session.

John emphasized the vital role of marketing and business development in shaping long-term strategic plans. He highlighted the necessity of a robust marketing vision, encompassing understanding customer needs, establishing brand identity, evolving strategies, and continuously analyzing marketing effectiveness. Providing personalized, efficient, and excellent Customer care is the hallmark of success.

*John stressed that the purpose of the marketing function is **"to act as an ambassador of the customer and foster ethical relationships by effective contract management and prompt services leading to Customer Success."*** He then turned to Aryan, asking for his perspective on marketing through a mythological lens.

Aryan drew a parallel between marketing and Indra from Hindu mythology, portraying him as the revered king of deities with vast and multifaceted qualities. Aryan suggested that marketing professionals focus on strategic decision-making, aiming to become market leaders with an exceptional brand image inspired by Indra's leadership. Before Aryan could proceed further, Dr. Markesic stopped him and requested that he share the mythological story of Indra Deva.

Mythological Story of Indra

Aryan said Hindu mythology weaves captivating tales rich with symbolism and profound insights. These stories delve into the lives of various Gods and Goddesses, portraying celestial beings with distinctly human qualities. This humanlike portrayal connects us to these divine entities, making us realize that the forces of good and evil reside within us. These narratives guide us to acknowledge and confront our internal struggles and empower us to nurture goodness within.

Lord Indra is the King of Swarga (Heaven), ruling over the Devas (Gods) in Hinduism. His significance extends to Buddhism and Jainism, portraying him as a guardian deity and the king of the first heaven, Saudharmakalpa (सौधर्मकल्प). Indra is also the God of Thunder and Lightning, as described in the Rigvedas. He wields the power to invoke storms, rain, and strong river currents. Indra's mythology is often compared to Indo-European deities like Zeus, Perun, Thor, and Jupiter.

One of the central episodes in Indra's saga revolves around his confrontation with the evil demon Vritra, who aimed to destroy the peace and happiness among human beings on Earth. Vritra, blessed with near invincibility, wreaked havoc by seizing control of the heavens and causing chaos among the gods. To restore balance and protect humanity, Indra sought a solution. He approached the selfless sage, Dadhichi, requesting the sacrifice of his life to forge a weapon, the Vajra, capable of defeating Vritra. Dadhichi willingly sacrificed himself, showcasing his selflessness for the well-being of humanity.

With the powerful Vajra crafted from the sage's spine, Indra engaged in a fierce battle with Vritra. The clash resulted in the demon's defeat, releasing the waters he had hoarded and rejuvenating the earth. By killing the Vritra,

Indra established himself as a friend of humanity, restoring peace, joy, and sunshine on this planet.

This victory symbolized the triumph of righteousness over arrogance, emphasizing the importance of self-sacrifice for cosmic welfare. Indra's stories reveal the nuanced complexities of power and responsibility in the divine realm.

Dr. Markesic was satisfied. She thanked Aryan and asked him to continue about the evolution of Marketing Polestar.

Evolution of Marketing Polestar

Aryan said that Indra's story is similar to encouraging initiatives for business growth, excellence in driving sales, and expanding market reach despite facing numerous challenges. Indra's symbolism of authority and inspiration aligns with the marketing team's role as an ambassador for the customer. He urged marketing professionals to excel with integrity and empathy and to act as vigorous customer advocates, leading initiatives, fostering brand loyalty, and delivering personalized financial services.

Indra is a swift, decisive, firm, and strong king of Devas. His actions can shake and disrupt the stable foundations of his adversaries. Even when leading a vast army of a hundred divisions, Indra's focused approach and unwavering determination enabled him to emerge victorious in battles. He signifies his warrior prowess and ability to overcome enemies through strength and strategic skill.

The discussion concluded the pre-lunch session with the finalization of the Marketing Polestar as,

"As Customer Ambassadors, we uphold integrity, empathy, and excellence, delivering

Empower Limitless Vision

personalized financial services and business solutions for Customer Success, stakeholder value, and universal well-being."

CEO John urged the group to plan measurable parameters and annual targets to track progress toward the marketing Polestar. The Head of Marketing, leading the group, finalized the following measurable parameters with yearly targets to attain the marketing polestar:

1. **<u>Brand Awareness and Loyalty</u>**: Track repeat customers, referral rates, and social media to ensure that brand awareness increases by 10% or more in the target market.

2. **<u>Net Promoter Score (NPS)</u>**: It measures customer loyalty by tracking positive customer recommendations to others. They set an annual target to increase NPS by 15%.

3. **<u>Customer Success</u>**: Measure customer satisfaction levels by conducting surveys twice a year and aim to increase the score by 10% during the year.

4. **<u>Response time</u>**: Monitor response time to customer inquiries and reduce it to under 24 hours.

5. **<u>Customized Financial Services</u>**: A 20% increase in customers receiving personalized financial services.

6. **<u>Customer Lifetime Value (CLTV)</u>:** Total value of critical customers, giving 80% business over the entire business relationship and increasing it by 20% annually.

7. **<u>Market share</u>**: Track the company's market share in relevant target markets and ensure an increase of 10% over the previous year.

8. **<u>Website Traffic:</u>** With the growing digital marketing, a target to measure the number of visitors to the company's website was set to increase by 10% annually.

9. **<u>Marketing ROI</u>**: The return on investment of marketing activities, a target value for marketing ROI, was set to achieve a ratio of 5:1 or higher.

10. **<u>Social Media Engagement:</u>** The level of engagement on social media platforms, such as likes, comments, and shares, ensures an increase of 5% annually.

The meeting concluded with the Head of Marketing expressing gratitude to everyone present. As pressure mounted on the remaining functions, plans were made for the next conference, focusing on the Technology function to finalize its vision and targets.

With this explanation, Aryan concluded his post-group meditation session discussions. Everyone was satisfied and left for his home.

-x-

Empower Limitless Vision

Engineering Polestar and Goddess Sarasvati

"OM, may we know Sarasvati. May we meditate on the daughter of Brahma, the Creator. May the Goddess illuminate our path and enlighten us."

- Sarasvati Gayatri Mantra

After Shruti's mother returned to India the following Saturday, Nancy thought of helping Shruti innovatively. She took the lead to a shared lunch after the post-meditation interactive session. She asked Dr. Markesic, Ramesh, Sophia, and other regular interaction participants to bring one dish each from their home for a shared lunch. It ensured that Shruti did not need to prepare food for the shared lunch at home. Shruti expressed her gratitude for this thoughtful gesture.

Ramesh arranged for the discussion recording to serve as a future reference, which impressed Dr. Markesic. She thanked Ramesh for this initiative. The closeness and warmth between Ramesh and Dr. Markesic were slowly rising. Interestingly, Dr. Shweta also participated in the interactive session followed by lunch, perhaps to build her opinion about the prospective matrimonial alliance between the two. She also blessed Aryan and Shruti for the success of their forthcoming venture.

Beginning the interaction from where they left off in their last meeting, Aryan said that three areas – Engineering, Technology, and Supply Chain Management, were left for evolving functional Polestars. In the absence of a coordinator for Engineering, Sophia took charge of organizing the meeting on March 6th, the Monday just before the Holi festival.

At the onset, the Head of Engineering welcomed all participants and thanked Sophia for organizing the full-day workshop to develop his function's Polestar and measurable parameters. He elaborated on the department's responsibilities, including designing, researching, and creating various products and services. It encompassed R&D for new technologies, process engineering and optimization, waste reduction, innovation, environmental impact reduction, new product development, reliability, researching market trends and consumer needs, and intellectual property management.

He emphasized the department's role in supporting other departments through training to foster a learning environment and invited CEO John to share his thoughts. John broadened his perspective on the department's role. He added that the purpose and objective of the department lie in **'designing products and services to achieve and maintain competitiveness in the market.'** Then John turned to Aryan, requesting his mythological insights for the department to facilitate the evolution of the Polestar.

Aryan drew a parallel, associating Goddess Sarasvati with the corporate functions of Research, Design, Knowledge Management, Learning, Fine Arts, and HRD, emphasizing the goddess's attributes of knowledge and creativity as most relevant to the department's role.

Before Aryan could proceed further, Dr. Markesic asked Aryan to share the mythological significance of the Sarasvati.

Significance of Goddess Sarasvati

Goddess Sarasvati has many names: Brahmani (power of Brahma), Brahmi (goddess of sciences), Bharadi (goddess of history), Vani and Vachi (both referring to the flow of music/song, melodious speech), Varnesvari (goddess of letters), Kavijihvagravasini (one who dwells on the tongue

Empower Limitless Vision

of poets), Vidyadatri (Goddess who provides knowledge), Veenavadini (Goddess who plays veena), Vagdevi (Goddess of speech), Pustakadharini (Goddess who carries a book), Veenapani (Goddess who has a veena), and Hamsavahini (Goddess who sits on swan). She is revered in Jainism and Buddhism as well. In the Upanishads, Goddess Sarasvati is invoked to meditate on the nature of virtue and virtuous actions.

Goddess Sarasvati illustrates the profound significance of knowledge, creativity, music, flowing water, abundance and wealth, art, speech, wisdom, and learning in the cosmic order. *The word "Sara" is translated as "Essence," and "Sva" is translated as "Self." Thus, Sarasvati would translate to "She who helps realize the essence of self" or "realize the essence (of Parabrahman) with one's self."* She symbolizes inspiration and guidance for seekers of wisdom and enlightenment.

The story goes that after creating the universe, Lord Brahma wanted to create life in it and realized that knowledge and wisdom were essential for the sustenance and order of the universe. In his quest to bring forth these divine qualities, Brahma created Goddess Sarasvati.

Legend states that Sarasvati was born from Brahma's mouth, symbolizing the divine origin of language, speech, and creative expression. She is often depicted as a graceful and ethereal deity, seated on a white lotus, wearing a white saree, and playing the veena, a musical instrument representing the harmony of creation.

Goddess Sarasvati is one of the Tridevi, and the goddesses Lakshmi and Parvati. Sarasvati is Lord Brahma's consort, the universe's creator, and the sister of Shiva. On the auspicious Vasant Panchami day (the fifth day of spring and known as Sarasvati Puja), students, writers, musicians, and anyone related to the field of knowledge worship Goddess Sarasvati. Small children begin to write alphabets on this sacred day to invoke her blessings for wisdom and academic excellence. With this, Aryan concluded his talk about the goddess. Overwhelmed with the narration, Dr. Markesic requested him to elaborate on how they evolved the Polestar.

Evolution of Engineering Polestar

Aryan replied that after briefly explaining the significance of Goddess Sarasvati during the meeting, he retreated from John's views that the purpose of the Engineering function lies in shaping the products to stay competitive in a dynamic market. To incorporate the virtues of Goddess Sarasvati into this vision, he highlighted the four points:

- <u>Knowledge and Wisdom</u>: It is necessary for learning, research, and intellectual excellence in designing innovative products and services.
- <u>Creativity and Innovation</u>: Building a culture of innovation within the Engineering department is essential for providing creative solutions, new technologies, and groundbreaking ideas.
- <u>Harmony and Balance</u>: For a harmonious integration of design elements, functionality, and sustainability in the products and services engineered by the department.
- <u>Expression and Communication</u>: Effective communication in the design process is essential for ensuring that the engineered products and services convey a clear and compelling message to the market.

It was followed by elaborate discussions and brainstorming for two hours, leading to the development of the following functional Polestar:

"Engineer innovative products and services, nurture a learning culture fostering creativity, and maintain design harmony for sustained market competitiveness."

As the CEO and most of the Functional Heads left the meeting after lunch, the Head of the Design & Development department chaired the post-lunch session to develop the following measurable parameters and annual targets for the company's Balanced Scorecard:

1. **New Patents:** To increase the number of filed patents by 20% over the previous year
2. **Training Hours per Employee:** An annual target of a 15% increase in average training hours per employee was kept to create a learning environment.
3. **Product Development Efficiency:** It was decided that the time taken from conceptualization to product launch should be reduced by 10%.
4. **Customer Satisfaction:** To achieve a minimum 90% customer satisfaction rating.
5. **Environmental Sustainability:** To attain a 5% reduction in the environmental impact of products annually.
6. **Artistic Elements in Products:** To enhance the aesthetic elements in at least 25% of new products.
7. **Cross-functional Integration:** To increase cross-functional collaboration by initiating at least two joint projects with other departments per year.
8. **Success rate of R&D projects:** To ensure good quality of Research and Development, achieve a success rate of 80% or higher for R&D projects.

9. **Creative Work Environment:** Maintain a minimum 85% employee satisfaction rating for the work environment's creativity support.

At the end of the meeting, the Head of Engineering thanked all participants. He concluded that the identified parameters and annual targets will ensure his department's success while drawing inspiration from Goddess Sarasvati.

Dr. Shweta was impressed by how Aryan integrated spiritual values into his professional life. She was unsure about the quantum of its impact on mental development and the Samskara of an unborn child. However, she was sure that the efforts made by parents would positively impact their children. Intrigued by the Polestar concept, she asked Aryan to share his views about the **Polestar for her nursing home.**

Aryan thought for a while and replied that it could **"Provide Personalised efficient and excellent Medical Care."** He added that you might draw inspiration from the virtues of Lord Dhanvantari to finetune it. Shruti said the word 'Medical care' may be modified to 'Maternal care.' Dr. Shweta and Dr. Markesic quickly noted all the points and decided to work on them.

Inspired by the discussion, Ramesh asked what could be a Polestar for a manufacturing company. Aryan thought for a while and said let us assume the company manufactures electronic products. Its Polestar could be **"Timely delivery of quality electronic products and services at an optimum cost with a continual improvement focus to ensure customer success."**

Ramesh exclaimed, Wonderful! "You have inbuilt all the four essential elements of Quality, Cost, Delivery, and Services in the statement to ensure Customer Success."

Nancy asked, what is the difference between customer satisfaction and customer success? Aryan replied that customer satisfaction means fulfilling customer needs. If you give a customer more than what he asked for, it is customer delight. For example, your idea of a shared lunch today, in which everyone brings an item from home, is a customer delight for us. As we never expected it as your customer. Customer Success is a step further, where you think beyond customer delight. It happens when you think about the success of customer's customers or stakeholders. The research by Dr. Markesic on little Rishi would help many young couples in the future. It is customer success.

Shruti said, let us stop discussions. Yummy food is waiting for all of you. They all enjoyed the lunch together and then returned to their homes with enhanced happiness.

-X-

Empower Limitless Vision

Technology Polestar and Agni Deva

We worship Agni, the divine priest of the sacrifice, the bestower of treasures, and the invoker of the gods.   *- Rigveda 1.1*

Aryan's preparations for opening his Consultancy Startup were in full swing. They celebrated little Rishi's fourth monthly milestone birthday on the 28th July at the orphanage. The next day, Saturday, group meditation was organized as usual at their home. Despite Aryan leaving the company, the Young Thinktank continued to look after the logistics and participated in the group meditation. Group meditation helped them to remain calm and internally happy.

In the subsequent meeting after the meditation, Aryan explained how they evolved the Technology Polestar and cultivated pious Samskara in Rishi. After finalizing the Polestar of most functions, two functions, Technology and Supply Chain Management, were left. Adam, the functional coordinator of Technology, made the necessary arrangements for the workshop to evolve the Technology Polestar.

Amidst preparations, the Holi festival arrived. There was little enthusiasm for celebrating the Indian festival in the USA as Holi fell on a Wednesday, 8th March, a working day. The local Indian community in New Jersey decided to organize the Holi festivities the following Sunday, and Aryan eagerly participated in the festival. In contrast, Shruti watched him and his celebrations, praying for her son to learn the essence of Holi celebrations and Indian cultural heritage, embodying the spirit of love and forgiveness

Empower Limitless Vision

towards others. Her mother and Mrs. Sharma were taking special care of Shruti at this stage of her pregnancy.

Dr. Markesic asked about the significance of the Holi festival. Shruti replied that the Holi festival has cultural relevance, similar to ***the festival of colors in India. It is the festive day to end and rid oneself of past errors, end conflicts by meeting others, and forget and forgive.*** People pay or forgive debts and deal anew with those in their lives. Today, when global conflicts are increasing, the celebration of Holi has become even more critical to preserve humanity. Shruti referred to the ongoing Russia-Ukraine war, where the NATO countries are supporting Ukraine. To peacefully resolve the conflicts, the nations need to adopt forgiveness and reconciliation in the true spirit of Holi. Holi is a potent reminder to foster understanding between individuals, communities, and countries. Listening to such beautiful thoughts from Shruti, Dr. Markesic started internally feeling that she had nurtured a divine soul in her son. Dr. Markesic requested that Aryan narrate the Technology Polestar story further.

Aryan subordinated the Head of Technology to the IT Manager before his transformative journey to the Himalayas. He felt indebted to him for his professional grooming. Aryan suggested that Adam organize a full-day meeting on Friday, 10th March, to wind up the exercise quickly. Drawing from the experience of other coordinators, Adam made all the necessary preparations and invited participants to the meeting.

The Technology Polestar formulation meeting, chaired by CEO John, was held on Friday as planned. To maintain momentum, all functional heads and Apex committee members participated in the conference. The

Empower Limitless Vision

functional coordinators supported each other during the session, with Aryan playing a pivotal role in driving them.

Welcoming the participants, the Head of Technology shared the critical responsibilities of the Information Technology (IT) Department. He elaborated that they manage IT infrastructure and systems, maintain network and cybersecurity, maintain software and hardware, ensure data storage and backup, and provide technical support and troubleshooting. He then invited the CEO to give opening remarks.

CEO John emphasized the need to evolve the Technology's functional Vision. The objective was to leverage emerging technologies, drive business agility, optimize processes, and ensure secure operations and environmental sustainability. He stressed addressing the following points in the **Technology Polestar:**

- *Ensure the State-of-the-art Technology, Software, and Capital Assets to maintain competitiveness.*
- *Enhance productivity with AI as far as possible to ensure continual technological improvement.*
- *Optimize the quality and ensure timely delivery of the products and services, leading to Customer Success.*

He emphasized identifying the measurable parameters and setting suitable targets for these parameters. John invited Aryan to share his mythological perspective on technology. Aryan said Technology is related to Agni Deva, the God of Fire. Before Aryan could proceed further, Dr. Markesic asked him to share the story of Agni Deva.

Story of Agni Deva

Aryan begins by narrating the Agni Gayatri mantra,

"OM, let me meditate on the great flame, O! God of fire, grant me a higher intellect. Let Agni Deva, the radiant God of Fire, illuminate my mind."

The first hymn of the oldest Hindu scripture, the Rigveda, invokes Agni Deva and praises Agni as the divine priest and bestower of offerings in the sacred ritual of yajna. It emphasizes his central role in maintaining cosmic order and facilitating communication between the earthly and celestial realms. Agni is born out of the cosmic waters and carries offerings from humans to the gods. Agni consumes the sacred Soma, a holy plant associated with immortality and enlightenment, and brings the Soma from Heaven to Earth.

Agni is often depicted with two faces, symbolizing his dual role as both the domestic hearth fire and the sacrificial fire. In creation stories, Agni represents the transformative power of fire in the cosmic cycle.

In the epics Ramayana and Mahabharata, Agni plays a crucial role. In the Ramayana, Agni helps Lord Rama by consuming the demoness Shurpanakha's body after Rama mutilates her. In the Mahabharata, Agni accepts the Khandava forest as an offering from Arjuna and Lord Krishna, clearing the way for the construction of Indraprastha.

Overall, the story of *Agni highlights the significance of fire in Hindu rituals, symbolizing purification, transformation, and the connection between the earthly and divine realms.*

Evolution of Technology Polestar

Aryan drew a parallel between the transformative power of technology and digitization and the deity Agni. Agni's role as an intermediary, purifier, and bestower of knowledge and blessings reflected technology's immense potential and positive impact on our lives. *Agni Deva represented the Fire of Digital Transformation, connecting humans to the divine, just as technology connects people in the digital realm. Agni symbolized the essential role of technology in facilitating communication, innovation, and progress, much like Agni's mediating attributes.*

Agni's presence throughout the heavens, earth, and atmosphere represented the omnipresence of technology and its transformative influence on every aspect of human life. Agni's ability to overcome obstacles aligns with technology's power to empower humans to overcome challenges through innovation, digitization, and artificial intelligence. Agni, the invoker, the bringer of truth, and the bestower of blessings, symbolized the need to harness emerging technologies, enhance digitization, and drive business agility. Inviting to join Agni emphasized the collaborative and interconnected nature of the digital world.

Agni illuminates cutting-edge technologies like Artificial Intelligence (AI) for business transformation. Agni signifies IT's responsibility for cybersecurity, securing, and safeguarding digital assets. After deliberation, the following Technology Polestar evolved:

"Drawing inspiration from Agni Deva, leverage State-of-the-Art Technology for agility, optimize processes, and deliver value-added services while ensuring secure global operations, cybersecurity, and environmental sustainability."

Empower Limitless Vision

During the post-lunch session, chaired by the Head of Technology, the following measurable parameters and annual targets to attain the Technology Polestar were set:

1. **Technology Adoption Rate:** Achieve a minimum adoption rate of 80% for emerging technologies across relevant departments and processes.

2. **Availability of IT Tools and Equipment:** Ensure 99.9% system uptime during the year.

3. **Digital Transformation Index:** Assess the level of technology and digitization across the company and aim for a 10% increase in the Index over the previous year.

4. **Cybersecurity Metrics:** Continuously maintain zero security vulnerabilities and security incidents per year.

5. **Process Optimization Metrics:** To reduce operations cost by 15% and increase productivity by 10% for key business processes

6. **Value-Added Services**: To get 10% revenue growth and ensure customer satisfaction ratings are above 90% through value-added services.

7. **Business Agility:** To respond to market fluctuations and reduce time-to-market for new products by 20%.

8. **Environmental Sustainability Metrics:** Undertake technology initiatives to minimize environmental impact and reduce energy consumption by 15%.

As Aryan ended his narration, Ramesh requested him to continue and share one more functional polestar. Dr. Markesic also supported the idea. Aryan shared the Supply Chain Management Polestar, thinking it would complete his narration of all polestars and allow him to focus on his forthcoming startup.

Supply Chain Polestar and Varuna Deva

"Oh, may we know the sphere of water? May we meditate on the Blue Being. May Varuna, the Lord of waters, illuminate our paths and enlighten us."

- Varuna Gayatri Mantra.

Aryan continued by saying that after finalizing the functional Polestar of all other functions, Supply Chain Management (SCM) was the only function left. No functional coordinator was present in SCM. Thus, Young Thinktank took the lead, worked together, and facilitated the SCM functional polestar evolution exercise on the last day of CEO John's deadline for all functions.

At the outset of the meeting, the Head of Supply Chain Management thanked Young Thinktank for organizing a full-day workshop to evolve Polestar for his function. He pledged to appoint his function's coordinator within a week and then explained the activities the SCM department undertakes.

He said Materials Management looked after planning, sourcing, purchasing, receiving, storing, and maintaining materials and product inventory for production or service delivery. It included coordination with the production planning and manufacturing departments. However, all these activities are only a subset of the SCM department activities.

SCM encompasses all activities related to sourcing, procurement, conversion, and logistics of goods and services. It involves the raw material procurement process, manufacturing and assembling products, and delivering them to customers. SCM is a holistic approach that includes all activities in getting a product or service from the supplier

Empower Limitless Vision

to the customer. Demand forecasting, sustainable sourcing of raw materials and components, and managing supplier relationships are critical for success. Then, he invited CEO John to share his perspective.

CEO John asked the Head of SCM to nominate a functional coordinator quickly to drive excellence initiatives in the function. The evolution of SCM Polestar is only the beginning. When setting his expectations, the CEO said that materials management is **"The right quality, right price, right quantity, at the right place, at the *right time."***

SCM includes the "Sustainability" of each activity from the supplier to the customer delivery, including sustainable relationships and availability of quality assets to perform desired operations. Then, he asked Aryan to share his mythological interpretation.

Aryan had become popular amongst colleagues for his mythological insights, and his admirers were growing. Aryan said that Kubera, the revered deity of wealth and prosperity, symbolically connects to raw materials and components and inventory management as the guardian of treasures and the manager of wealth and resources. Kubera's association with abundance may lead to excess inventory and storage.

In Supply Chain Management, the "FLOW" is paramount. Flow is the virtue of Varuna Deva. *Thus, the functional polestar of the SCM is driven by Varuna Deva to create a streamlined and sustainable supply chain from supplier to customer delivery. Varuna Deva maintains the flow of materials, components, finished goods, etc., and ensures the availability of the right quality resources in the correct quantity at the right place and time. For example, the Ganga continuously flows from the Himalayas to Gangasagar and culminates in the sea. Any* obstruction in its flow may lead to floods and other problems. Aryan then narrated the story of Varuna.

Story of Varuna Deva

Varuna is the deity associated with the ocean, rivers, and atmospheric phenomena. In Hindu mythology, Varuna's character symbolizes the intricate balance between cosmic order, justice, and the eternal cycle of life. *A hymn of the Yajur Veda says,* **"Varuna is Vishnu, and Vishnu is Varuna."** As per the Rigveda, Varuna ensures the implementation of moral laws, punishing the remorseless and forgiving the repentant.

Varuna is often paired with Mitra, forming a divine duo. Mitra is associated with the day, while Varuna is linked with the night. Together, they represent the duality of time and cosmic balance. The story of Varuna revolves around his role as the god or the source of all heavenly waters, overseeing his abode, Vārunānī, the celestial ocean that encircles the universe. *The name Váruna is derived from the Sanskrit root vr, meaning "to surround, to cover" or "to restrain, bind," signifying his connection to the cosmic ocean and the binding force of universal law or Rta. As the guardian of Rta, the cosmic order that governs the universe, Varuna ensures that everything in the cosmos functions in harmony and accordance with divine principles.*

Varuna is often portrayed as a god of justice, watching over the deeds of mortals. He is omniscient and all-seeing, aware of every action and thought. Varuna is associated with Dharma, the concept of righteous conduct, and Vedic hymns invoke him seeking forgiveness for transgressions. Dr. Markesic was happy to understand the significance of Varuna and requested that Aryan share about the SCM Polestar.

Empower Limitless Vision

Supply Chain Management Polestar

Varuna Deva is associated with the cosmic order and cosmic law and symbolizes the balance of natural forces aligned with the intricate dynamics of SCM. The flow of materials in any system involves maintaining equilibrium, much like the cosmic balance upheld by Varuna. The deity's influence is reflected in a structured and regulated flow in SCM.

Varuna signifies ethical conduct, which is crucial for effective SCM. As Varuna is the guardian of cosmic order, SCM must ensure the orderly movement of resources, promoting transparency and accountability at every stage. Furthermore, Varuna's association with water, often depicted with a noose, signifies control and regulation. In SCM, control over the flow of materials is imperative, ensuring a streamlined process from procurement to distribution. Varuna's noose represents the need for restraint and responsible utilization, emphasizing the importance of avoiding waste and inefficiency in SCM.

After detailed discussions, the group finalized the following functional Polestar for Supply Chain Management:

"To ensure cost-effective availability of quality materials and assets to nurture a Seamless and Sustainable Ethical Material Flow for Global Financial Eminence and Stakeholder Well-being."

John and other functional heads left the meeting during the lunch break, and the Head of SCM chaired the discussion in the post-lunch session. They identified the following parameters and annual targets to accomplish the functional vision of Supply Chain Management. The measurable parameters focused on optimizing the flow of materials, minimizing waste, and ensuring ethical practices throughout the SCM function.

1. **Material Waste Reduction:** To promote sustainability, reduce material waste by 10% across the supply chain.
2. **On-Time Delivery Performance:** Ensure timely material flow to ensure 95% on-time delivery of raw materials, components, and finished goods as per plan.
3. **Ethical Sourcing Compliance:** Ensure that 90% of materials sourced from suppliers adhere to ethical and sustainable practices.
4. **Inventory Turnover Ratio**: An annual target of 12 inventory turns was kept to manage the inventory efficiently with an aspiration to improve further by 10%.
5. **Supplier Performance**: Cultivate partnership relations with suppliers while maintaining a supplier performance index comprising delivery time, product quality, cost, and customer service above 95%
6. **Order Accuracy**: Achieve an order accuracy rate of 99% or above during the year.
7. **Total Cost of Ownership**: Reduce costs of acquiring materials, including transportation, storage, and handling charges, by 5% compared to the previous year through streamlined processes and optimized resource utilization.
8. **Stockout Rate**: Keep the stockout rate below 1%.
9. **Well-being of Mankind**: Achieve 100% compliance with all relevant environmental regulations and implement two new projects to reduce the environmental impact of materials management each year.
10. **Sustainability metrics:** Continuously monitor and work towards reducing the carbon footprint, improving waste management, and adopting eco-friendly practices.

The Head of SCM thanked all coordinators, especially Aryan, for organizing the workshop. He promised to appoint a suitable coordinator for SCM soon. Everyone was happy after completing the task of developing the functional polestar for all significant functions as scheduled.

CEO John, expressing his happiness and satisfaction, asked Aryan to organize the Apex Thinktank meeting. While praising Aryan and Young Thinktank for completing the innovative exercise of aligning the functional polestars with the company's vision on time, the members of Apex Thinktank reviewed the future course of action. John said it was a critical milestone toward success. He instructed all concerned to incorporate the measurement parameters identified into the functional and company's Balanced Score Card for the next fiscal. He emphasized the importance of monthly monitoring of annual plans to identify any deviations and make necessary corrections. Well-defined processes would ensure optimal resource utilization, minimal waste, reduced operational costs, and improved profitability. He asked everyone to focus on the current financial year targets for the remaining fifteen days of the fiscal year. With this, Aryan concluded his story about aligning his official accomplishments with his aspirations to invoke a Corporate Guru in their unborn son during Shruti's eighth and ninth months of pregnancy.

Dr. Markesic, Ramesh, and other participants thanked Aryan for helping them understand the new learning. Dr. Markesic said let us keep one more session on the first Saturday of August as the concluding session to focus on any unanswered doubts and questions. Aryan happily agreed to her proposal, and they closed the discussion for the day.

-x-

Empower Limitless Vision

Chapter 4: Achieve Everlasting Success

Self-Inspiration through Daily Affirmation

Device Motivational Measurement Parameters

Ancient Secrets of Everlasting Success

The Journey Continues...

Self-Inspiration through Daily Affirmation

"Let noble thoughts come to us from every side."   - Rig Veda 1.89.1

After several post-meditation meetings, Dr. Markesic and Ramesh grew closer. After getting most of the inputs, including the Functional Polestars, Dr. Markesic requested one more meeting on Saturday, August 6th, to address the remaining queries. She spent two days reviewing her notes and identifying the gaps in her input.

On Saturday, when they met post-group meditation, Ramesh looked happy. He announced his affirmation of participating in group meditation regularly. He felt benefited from meditation in the past two months. It triggered Dr. Markesic to make a similar commitment. Observing both with love, Aryan and Shruti looked at each other, smiled, and welcomed them as regular participants in the group meditation. Internally, all of them knew the hidden purpose of joining group meditation. Sometimes, such positive decisions bring extraordinary enjoyment in life.

Driven by these responses, Dr. Markesic inquired about the benefits of linking functional polestars with Hindu deities. Aryan emphasized that despite distinct characteristics, all Gods share inherent qualities, such as universal well-being. Focusing on this quality in corporate pursuits could make the world happier, fostering care for one another. The functional polestar serves as intrinsic self-affirmation for this vision.

Dr. Markesic inquired about individuals and whether they should link themselves with specific deities. Aryan explained that traditionally, a Guru imparts a Guru mantra to disciples, who then use it as a daily self-

affirmation to embody the virtues of the deity. Disciples align their professions with the mantra's essence or the deity's skills, practicing divine virtues to move toward salvation.

When asked how a functional polestar motivates employees, **Aryan emphasized that each polestar carries a message of universal well-being alongside the function's vision. It is a daily affirmation, encouraging employees to strive for excellence and connect with the cosmos, the source of infinite energy.** However, achieving excellence depends on adequate resources, role model behavior, work culture, skills, work plan, and monitoring mechanisms. The functional polestar is a catalyst, guiding employees in the right direction."

Ramesh inquired about the significance of parental Brahmacharya in invoking a divine soul, questioning its limited endorsement in medical research. Aryan explained that Nature has universally imposed Brahmacharya (sexual restraint) on all species except humans. Without such restraint, the planet would witness an uncontrollable population explosion. Ancient wisdom advocates this practice, highlighting humanity's unique role in adhering to self-discipline for the upward flow of divine energy. This connection to the cosmos brings a natural radiance and extraordinary capabilities. While medical science may not fully grasp this concept, Aryan pointed to the radiant face of Rishi as an example of accumulated divine energy through self-discipline.

*A participant from the corporate communication field asked about the deity linked to his work. Shruti identified **Deva-rishi Narada and suggested a functional polestar for his area to "enhance and sustain the company's image as an ethical enterprise."***

Empower Limitless Vision

Dr. Markesic inquired from Aryan about the events following the finalization of the functional polestars in mid-March. Aryan explained that amidst the high pressure of fiscal year-end tasks, his primary focus was ensuring Shruti's well-being during the last few days of her pregnancy. All functions had established measurable parameters for their respective Functional Polestars, and the company's Balanced Scorecard for the next fiscal year was already in place. John had delegated the finalization of each function's Balanced Scorecard, cascading from the company's BSC and Functional Polestars to the Heads of Functions by the end of March. Meanwhile, Rishi was born on March 28th, prompting Aryan to take a three-week paternity leave.

During Aryan's absence, Apex Thinktank reviewed each function's Balanced Scorecard in the first fortnight of April, with Sophia coordinating in his place. Apart from routine activities, there were no significant developments. Dr. Markesic questioned why John had requested Aryan to continue until the first quarterly results. Aryan explained that John was uncertain about the impact of the Functional Polestars on the company's performance and wanted Aryan to guide individual functions on their subsequent actions. Moreover, finding a suitable substitute was challenging, and John believed Aryan could assist. To ensure continuity in the change management initiatives, John proposed that Aryan become the company's consultant upon starting his startup.

As Aryan prepared to leave, Victor organized a pivotal Apex Thinktank meeting to bid him farewell. Chaired by CEO John, the committee, including heads of HR, Finance, Quality, and Aryan, discussed concerns about the company's quarterly performance. High inflation in the USA and Europe was a critical reason for unfavorable results. Aryan's departure prompted Sophia's entry into the committee. Aryan, although silent during the meeting, later met with CEO John to share comprehensive solutions for change management. Recognizing the need for their solutions, John requested Aryan to be a consultant for the company, marking a win-win situation.

A grand farewell organized by the Young Thinktank celebrated Aryan's contributions, with CEO John announcing their consultancy commitment to him. Aryan's first assignment after launching his startup would be to assist the company in navigating its challenges.

Wrapping up the final interaction, Dr. Markesic expressed gratitude for the valuable insights on her research and personal growth gained from the sessions. Intrigued, she inquired about Aryan and Shruti's sentiments during the discussions. Glancing at Rishi's cheerful face, Shruti shared that the sessions had reinforced her dedication to universal well-being. *Aryan, nodding in agreement, considered it a divine blessing for Rishi, paving the way for his journey to become a Corporate Guru to guide the corporate world on a righteous path in an age dominated by money.* This newfound clarity inspired Aryan to name his consultancy startup **'Himalayan Insights,'** symbolizing a new era of change influenced by the blessings of Himalayan sages. Aryan and Shruti commended Dr. Markesic for her well-prepared and thoughtful questions, acknowledging her pivotal role in providing clarity for little Rishi and considering her an integral part of their family.

Dr. Markesic, touched by Aryan's reassurance and feeling the warmth of joy and love, pledged her commitment to regularly participate in the weekly group meditation sessions for research purposes and to foster a positive environment. With these sentiments, they concluded the session for the day, appreciating the shared journey of insights and personal growth.

-X-

Motivational Measurement Parameters

"Harmony in work and purpose is the key to motivation. Align your actions with the rhythm of your inner self, and you will find success metrics in the melody of your efforts."   - Sama Veda.

After Aryan left his lucrative job, he and Shruti found themselves jobless. However, they were financially secure, with enough savings to sustain a decent lifestyle for a year. They had diligently prepared to establish their upcoming startup consultancy firm, 'Himalayan Insights.' Aryan quickly completed the remaining formalities for the startup registration and opening. He designated the front room of their New Jersey residence as the company's registered office, with Shruti and himself as the two founding directors.

Interestingly, this room also served as their weekly group meditation space. They made minimal adjustments to the room's layout, placing a table with two chairs for the Directors in a corner. Previously used to distribute Prasada and breakfast after group meditation, this table retained its original purpose. Clients visiting for meetings had to remove their shoes outside before entering this registered office cum meditation room.

Clients could meditate with Aryan and Shruti before business discussions, either across the table or on the well-cushioned floor with backrests on the walls. This unique approach minimized expenses and attracted prospective customers to experience meditation during office visits. It ensured they entered discussions with a calm and affirmative mindset, leaving their worries behind. Positive vibes in the room were an additional advantage for them.

Determining Consultancy Charges

A few days later, Aryan revisited his former company to meet with HR Head Victor and Finance Head Thomas to discuss his consultancy assignment. It had been nearly a month since he left his position there, but this time, he returned in a different capacity—as a consultant. Despite the change in role, old connections persisted. In candid conversations, Victor shared that Aryan's departure had posed challenges for admirers and detractors. Despite grooming Sophia to take on Aryan's responsibilities, the senior-level void he left behind could not be filled.

Feeling a bit perplexed about setting his consultancy charges, Aryan inquired, "How do I determine my consultancy fees?" Thomas responded, emphasizing the need to consider various factors when deciding on a consulting rate. He advised Aryan to calculate his hourly rate based on his experience and industry standards. The suggested method involved dividing his former annual salary by 52 work weeks and then dividing that by 40 work hours per week to derive the previous hourly rate. However, Thomas cautioned that this rate didn't account for holidays, medical insurance, marketing expenses, research time before providing services, and other miscellaneous costs.

In addition to factoring in time, Thomas advised Aryan to consider additional costs that might arise during his consultancy, such as expenses on materials, project-related transport, office rent, logistic costs, business disruptions, and unforeseen expenses. Thomas suggested a rough estimate, mentioning that if Aryan had an annual package of $200k, his hourly rate would be $200. Depending on the industry and services, a 20 to 30% higher charge might be applicable. Market and competitor prices were also key considerations, with a recommendation not to exceed a 25-30 percent markup.

After accounting for the time estimate and additional costs, Thomas urged Aryan to choose a pricing model based on the project's nature, the client's preferences, and the structure that would ensure fair compensation. **The fundamental principle, however, was that the client should receive benefits at least five times the payment made to Aryan.**

Considering all these factors, they collectively formulated a mutually beneficial consultancy fee structure, solidifying an agreement based on a per-day engagement model for a minimum of 40 days per year.

Expressing gratitude, Aryan thanked Victor and Thomas for their invaluable advice and suggestions. Subsequently, they convened with CEO John, who conveyed his satisfaction with the contract's finalization. John recommended that Aryan commence his work with them the next day, emphasizing his role in guiding the top management team through a review of 'Change Management' initiatives. Sophia was asked to assist Aryan with the task, as she had been doing before. Aryan's former office had been converted into a temporary workspace for the consultant. Aryan decided to kick off his initial three-day assignment starting on Monday.

Essentials for Change Management

On Monday morning, Aryan was back in his cabin after a month, but in a different role as a consultant. Sophia eagerly anticipated Aryan's visit would provide her with invaluable insights and fruitful outcomes under his guidance. Before dispensing advice, Aryan requested Sophia to coordinate one-on-one meetings with all department heads, followed by sessions with a cross-section of executives from each function. Each meeting and interactive session was planned for 30 to 45 minutes. Swiftly organizing these sessions,

Sophia aimed to be present in each meeting, taking notes and absorbing insights from Aryan.

While Sophia arranged the meetings, Aryan prepared his discussion points for each function. Additionally, he instructed each department to share their Balanced Scorecards for the year, providing a status update on each point. The extensive series of meetings and data collection spanned two full days. Aryan delved into the detailed data, identifying new insights to present on the third day. He instructed Sophia to arrange a meeting of all department heads, chaired by CEO John, to share his feedback. Given that this was his inaugural consultancy assignment, much was at stake for Aryan. At home, he meditated with Shruti to crystallize his ideas and diligently prepared a presentation.

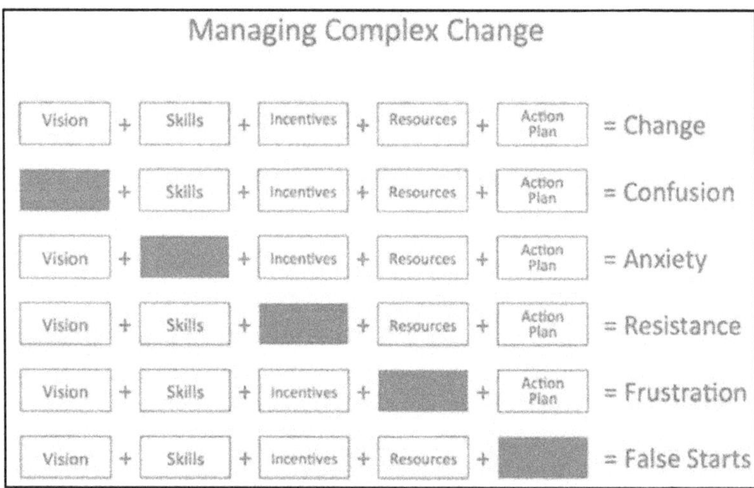

On the third day, during the feedback meeting led by CEO John, Aryan shared the Knoster model for "Managing Complex Change," developed by Knoster, Villa, and

Thousand (2000), a model widely applied in diverse contexts. According to this model:

Vision + Skills + Incentives + Resources + Action Plan = Change

Without any of these five essential elements (Vision, Skill, Incentives, Resources, and Action Plan), the desired change will not materialize. Instead, it may lead to confusion, anxiety, resistance, frustration, or a false start. Drawing from interactions and data analysis, Aryan provided examples illustrating how the absence or inadequacy of each parameter in different parameters contributed to problems and issues during implementation.

Aryan observed that the confusion regarding the need for a cultural shift and growth significantly diminished as the functional vision evolved and became well-understood. However, a lack of skills to drive change resulted in anxiety among members of the top management team. To address this anxiety, companies often enlist the help of consultants. Yet, Aryan pointed out that consultants, while helpful, may lack insight into the company's internal dynamics and work culture, requiring substantial data to draw meaningful conclusions.

He recommended that each functional area scrutinize all parameters where results fell short of expectations. Aryan underscored the overall outcome, emphasizing that insufficient incentives are a significant root cause of resistance to change. He suggested measures to enhance employee engagement and motivation to mitigate this. Concerns about resources and action planning were minimal and could be addressed individually.

John highly appreciated the in-depth analysis presented by Aryan. He added that Aryan had groomed Sophia and that she was doing a good job. After the conclusion of the meeting, Aryan had a one-to-one meeting

Empower Limitless Vision

with John. Aryan explained specific critical reasons for employee resistance to driving cultural change. John also inquired about Aryan's consultancy business. Aryan replied that he had received some business queries from other potential customers, including one from Shruti's previous employer's client from Chicago. However, it may take some time to materialize. John asked Aryan to provide his services three to four days a month to review the status of their excellence journey. He desired that Aryan plan his next visit within two weeks and help them develop the metrics of inspiration.

Motivational Performance Metrics

Aryan was happy with the successful inaugural three-day consultancy assignment and another two-day visit assignment in the pipeline. In addition, he had an assured business of monthly follow-ups at his previous company. At home, he discussed the outcomes with Shruti and sought her suggestions on contemplating the profound impact of motivation or inspiration.

Together, they agreed that motivation is the driving force to bring requisite change in individual and collective achievements. It is a critical factor for personal and professional success. The intent and design of measurement parameters are vital in harnessing and enhancing motivation. These parameters are instruments capable of spreading positivity and motivating individuals and teams to move forward. Shruti emphasized the importance of evaluation parameters: **"If you measure the right things, the right results will follow. If you measure the wrong things, wrong results will follow."**

Setting aspirational personal and professional goals with tangible indicators of accomplishment is a primary motivational parameter at an individual level. Such goals offer valuable insights into an individual's drive, whether

Empower Limitless Vision

achieved through completing tasks, reaching milestones, or realizing aspirations.

For a company, they evolved a concept of "Motivational Metrics," highlighting the positive reinforcement approach, such as measures like "You have almost completed the task; 95% of the work completed; Wonderful! Keep it up!!" that motivate an employee. Conversely, demotivating metrics might negatively express the same performance shortfall, such as "You failed by 5%. Once again, you could not complete the task." They felt that metrics used in the Balanced Scorecard and Annual Performance Appraisal should be critically examined to keep everyone motivated and enhance employee morale. ***Metrics of Inspiration lead to higher levels of engagement, a motivated workforce, increased participation in improvement initiatives, teamwork, and improved overall satisfaction. It contributes to gauging the motivational pulse of a company.***

To further explore the motivational power of setting aspirational targets and offering constructive feedback, rewards, and recognition to employees, Aryan conducted a two-day consultancy assignment at his former company after a few days. Addressing the top management team, he emphasized the need for regular recognition, especially public acknowledgment, to foster an appreciation culture. **The most effective recognition lies in enhancing an employee's reputation in the eyes of family and close associates. Intrinsic satisfaction is crucial, derived from aligning tasks with personal values and finding purpose and enjoyment in one's job. Learning and Development Opportunities play a significant role in motivating employees, and metrics related to training participation and skill acquisition demonstrate their impact. Lastly, balancing professional responsibilities and**

Empower Limitless Vision

personal well-being, known as Work-Life Balance, is essential for sustained motivation.

He concluded that organizations that invest in ethical working witness a surge in motivation in their employees' growth and skill enhancement. He recommended specific changes in existing measurable parameters, and John was pleased to gain new insights from Aryan's visit, ensuring a win-win situation despite Aryan's departure.

Motivational Performance Metrics *at individual and organizational levels are indispensable for understanding, nurturing, and leveraging driving forces leading to personal and collective success.* Aryan got new insights for consultancy while going through the transformation process. Ever since Aryan and Shruti returned from the Himalayas, they have been a beacon of inspiration and a source of bliss. This influence has nurtured and guided their son, Rishi, since Shruti conceived him.

The fourth book of the "Corporate Transformation Series" will intricately explore the Motivation Mantra as its key focus area. It will contemplate the existing motivation theories and highlight new insights into motivation inspired by the Gayatri Mantra.

-x-

Ancient Secrets of Everlasting Success

Let us live in harmony, united in purpose, speaking with one voice.

- Atharva Veda 6.64.1

The two consecutive consultancy assignments, a total of five days of engagement during August, enabled Aryan to earn almost eighty percent of his earlier monthly salary in the first month of his consultancy startup. He considered keeping his target of an average of ten consultancy days, as he would spend almost equal time on the marketing and research work for the assignments received. He was feeling thankful to John. Soon after, Aryan and Shruti celebrated Rishi's fifth monthly milestone birthday at the orphanage in New Jersey and sponsored lunch for children. It was followed by the Annaprashana Samskar ritual on 2nd September, immediately after Saturday's group meditation.

Annaprashana Samskara is a traditional Hindu ritual that introduces solid foods to an infant's diet when the child is five to six months of age. It involved purification rituals to invoke the blessings of deities and Yagna under the guidance of Mrs Sharma. Mrs. Sharma also fed Rishi with his first solid bite, marking the transition from exclusive breastfeeding to the introduction of solid foods - a mixture of rice and other grains cooked with ghee and other auspicious ingredients. Aryan invited John, Victor, Thomas, Young Thinktank, Dr. Shweta, Dr. Markesic, Nancy, and Ramesh for this traditional celebration, followed by lunch, fostering a sense of joy.

While enjoying the lunch, John suggested that Aryan maintain a work-life balance as a key to happy living. Sharing his plans, **Aryan replied, Rig Veda explains the Rta, or cosmic order, stating that physical and moral laws govern the entire universe and that no**

transgression of these laws is allowed. He wanted to keep this teaching as the prime focus of his consultancy startup. His mission was to facilitate the corporate world to drive excellence while focusing on a Common Vision, Universal brotherhood, and Equitable Prosperity for all. Excellence lies in balancing and satisfying the needs of all stakeholders, including employees, customers, suppliers, shareholders, and society in general.

Amid contemporary self-help trends, ancient wisdom remains valuable, offering profound insights into success and fulfilling life. The knowledge from diverse cultures and traditions provides deep insights into success and a happy life. **One such timeless principle is the emphasis on balance and harmony, rooted in Eastern philosophies** like Taoism and the teachings of ancient Greek thinkers. Ancient Indian sages, philosophers, and thinkers have propagated the enduring principle of balance and harmony, which spans work and leisure, ambition and contentment, and material pursuits and spiritual well-being. Achieving life equilibrium is deemed foundational for sustained success.

For everlasting success, ancient wisdom encourages us to explore the depths of our consciousness and foster a sense of clarity, focus, and emotional resilience. Mindfulness and self-awareness find contemporary acclaim. Practices like meditation and Stoic philosophy underscore the importance of understanding oneself, mastering the mind, and fostering inner peace. *The principle of 'Dharma,' or one's righteous duty, deeply ingrained in Indian philosophy, provides a roadmap for a purposeful and successful life. By **aligning our actions with higher values and contributing positively to the greater good**, we echo purpose-driven living, where success transcends personal gain to embrace a meaningful contribution to society.*

Aryan and Shruti incorporated these precious learnings as a unique feature of their consultancy business, aiming to resolve business challenges using meditation and ancient wisdom for success. **Ancient wisdom underlines the significance of righteousness, continuous learning, and adaptability for growth.** Realizing that their clients in the USA may be believers of multiple faiths and may not be satisfied with Indian meditation practices, they studied other religious texts and ancient traditions. The famous quote by the Greek philosopher Heraclitus, ***"Change is the only constant,"*** encapsulated their quest for learning. They felt that embracing change, learning from experiences, and adapting to evolving circumstances are vital for sustained success.

Universal Model of Governance

Aryan had already intuitively derived the *'Universal Model of Governance'* by synthesizing a hymn from Rig-Veda (3-2-24-1), which states:

"Ye man! You need a governing body with three wings: Administrative Council (Rajya Sabha), Wisdom Council (Vidhya Sabha), and Ethics Council (Dharma Sabha). These councils approve all decisions so that you win over all situations fruitfully."

Swami Dayananda Sarasvati initially decoded the Universal Model of Governance (UMG) from the Rig-Veda. *Aryan was inclined to refer to one of his books and get its insights to further elaborate pictorially in the contemporary context with a detailed elaboration of the three councils' activities, responsibilities, and limitations.* ***UMG consists of three essential wings: the Administrative Council (Rajya Sabha), the Wisdom Council (Vidhya Sabha), and the Ethics Council (Dharma Sabha).*** *In a company, the*

Empower Limitless Vision

Administrative Council represents the top management team led by the CEO and is responsible for day-to-day operations and long-term strategic decisions. However, the Wisdom Council and Ethics Council need strengthening. The Wisdom Council's role is to enhance the stakeholders' skills and competencies, while the Ethics Council promotes values-based decision-making. The three councils administer control over one another to ensure that the other two councils operate within the boundaries set by one council. The CEO is a member of all three councils and must ensure unbiased and ethical decisions for the organization's long-term success.

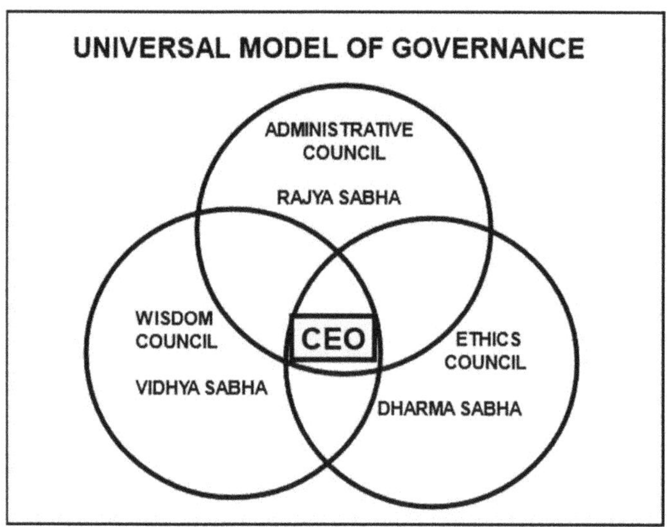

Aryan believes that the Rajya Sabha symbolizes Lord Vishnu with Goddess Laxmi, the Vidhya Sabha represents Lord Brahma with Goddess Sarasvati, and the Dharam Sabha plays the role of Lord Shiva with Goddess Parvati. Thus, the CEO or the king should have the qualities of the Trinity. In most companies, the leadership team is the Rajya

Empower Limitless Vision

Sabha or the Administrative Council. Independent Directors on the Board and Heads of Functions like Quality, Vigilance, Audits, Systems, etc., play the role of Dharma Sabha or Ethics Council to a varied degree of success and operational independence. Similarly, Heads of R&D, Design, learning, etc., play the role of Vidhya Sabha or Wisdom Council. Most companies need to strengthen the Wisdom Council and Ethics Council.

The importance of resilience and perseverance is woven into the fabric of ancient teachings. The story of the phoenix rising from its ashes, found in various mythologies, symbolizes the ability to overcome challenges and emerge stronger. From African proverbs to Native American teachings, ancient cultures emphasize the strength derived from ethical conduct. Indian ethos emphasizes, ***"Honesty is the Best Policy."*** Success is not a solitary pursuit but a collective journey where shared values and support enhance individual achievements.

Wisdom Council emphasizes building a learning environment. A conducive work environment free from fears is essential to motivate employees and other stakeholders to unleash their hidden potential and skills. Celebrating even the failures paves the way for a renewed zeal to work harder to succeed. The Stoic philosophy, emphasizing enduring hardships with equanimity, echoes this sentiment, highlighting that setbacks are not roadblocks but stepping stones to success.

Ancient teachings provide a treasure trove of wisdom transcending time and cultural boundaries. Rig Veda, the most ancient book on the earth, concludes with Sangathana Sukta. The soul of management science resides in the Sangthana Sukta, where the essence of ethics, wisdom, and administration culminate and enlighten humankind. It provides a new insight for the

business world to operate not as competitors but as collaborators with mutual trust, cooperation, and sharing to ensure the well-being of humankind.

Sangathan Sukta – A New World Order

The Rig Veda, the oldest sacred book in Hinduism with around 10,600 hymns, talks about prayers to deities, cosmic ideas, and philosophy. It envisions a world where people live happily, doing selfless deeds for others every day, like a mother caring for her child.

The concluding hymns of the Rig Veda, the Sangathan Sukta, are about creating a society where everyone's needs are met, higher values are respected, and everyone contributes to learning culture. It aims to nurture eternal happiness. Vedic teachings stress managing oneself and being disciplined, encouraging people to follow their duties (Swa-Dharma) for personal and societal well-being.

Aryan and Shruti were devoted to living this as role models. Vedic teachings guide us to align with cosmic laws. Sangathan Sukta's hymns outline a profound vision for a harmonious New World Order. It talks about universal brotherhood, harmony, love, and prosperity for everyone. The hymn says,

> *"O ye mankind! Let your vision & thinking of life be one and common, let your hearts be filled with equality, let your minds be united, resulting in equal prosperity & common excellence in life for all."*
> *– Sangathan Sukta, Rig Veda.*

The above hymn shows a new path to contemporary management science. This vision seeks unity, cooperation, and recognition of all beings' divinity. It imagines a business world where all stakeholders—suppliers, customers,

Empower Limitless Vision

employees, shareholders, competitors, and society—share a common vision. Their hearts are filled with mutual love, and their minds are united. Even competitors share technologies, research, and learning with mutual love, ensuring growth for all. Educational institutions, research labs, and businesses work together for society's larger good. The hymn assures everyone that this way of working leads to excellence, happiness, and prosperity. It echoes the new concepts for sustainable business through ethical living, social harmony, and knowledge pursuit for universal well-being. Sangathan Sukta ensures the wealth of the Greater Society. Competitors, customers, suppliers, educational institutions, and society follow ethical values, share knowledge, collaborate, and work towards a common vision for a sustainable, environment-friendly, happier, healthier, and prosperous world.

Aryan planned to spread these ideas through his startup, wanting his son Rishi to become a Corporate Guru—a universal role model for society. Aryan and Shruti lived and promoted these ancient teachings to ensure enduring principles of balance, mindfulness, purpose, adaptability, community, and resilience continue guiding the corporate world to success and inner happiness.

In a world full of fast changes and complexities, these timeless teachings offer a way to navigate life's challenges and uncertainties and find success. With these preparations, Aryan and Shruti entered a new era of life.

-x-

The Journey Continues...

"O man! Let equality prevail in your thoughts and attain wisdom. Let as equals carry further pondering; Prosperity blessed to you all is equal."

– Rig Veda.

A few days later, Aryan and Shruti sought tranquility along the Hudson River, opting for a serene afternoon. They wandered through the enchanting Hudson River Park, and Rishi was cradled in a comfortable baby carrier. Pausing at Pier 45, the family relished Rishi's joyful gurgles in response to the lively waterfront activities. The trio enjoyed a romantic stroll, embracing the summer and fall seasonal shifts. Amid the soothing sounds of a nearby fountain, they indulged in a leisurely meal.

With Rishi peacefully asleep, Aryan and Shruti sat on the grass. Delving into deep memory lane, Aryan, grateful for life's twists, pondered the significant changes over the past few years. The journey, marked by challenges and triumphs, joy and sorrow, love and pain, offered profound insights into life's mysteries. Aryan reminisced about his trajectory since joining a Financial Services MNC as a manager in 2018 after his Stanford MBA. His hard work and dedication led to his promotion after a year, accompanied by increased responsibilities and material success, symbolized by the gleaming Ferrari he acquired on his birthday—a glorious moment in his career growth journey. Soon after, Aryan suffered a severe COVID-19, when it spread in New York. He shared how neighbor Nancy cared for him, endearing herself to his parents. Though aware of the narration, Shruti relished realizing some unknown facets of life.

A touch of emotion surfaced as Aryan spoke of his parents' demise in the second wave of COVID-19 in New Delhi. However, this tragedy paved the way for Shruti to take care of his parents selflessly and silently enter his life as a twist in destiny. Grieved, Aryan sought solace in the Himalayas, where a sage not only lifted his depression but also orchestrated a transformative journey. Emerging from despair, Aryan serendipitously reunited with Shruti mystically. The Himalayan sage revealed that Aryan's parents had silently desired Shruti as their daughter-in-law, a sentiment unexpressed before their passing.

Aryan and Shruti, initially soulmates, evolved through shared meditation, embracing challenges and brahmacharya before becoming a married couple. Maintaining restraint even after marriage, they went through challenging penance for six months before conceiving a pious soul as their son, strictly following the ancient Hindu rituals. They eventually welcomed their son Rishi, who had a bright aura and was envisioned as a guiding force—a Corporate Guru—leading the business world on a righteous path. Impressed by their amazing story, a young gynecologist, Dr. Markesic, took a research project to study how they could teach the desired Values and virtues in their son Rishi, even before conceiving and during pregnancy.

Despite jeopardizing their careers, Shruti devoted two years to childcare leave, followed by six months of maternity leave. Aryan also left his lucrative job and launched the consultancy startup *Himalayan Insights*. Despite securing a few assignments and long-term agreements, Aryan struggled to establish his startup and devoted considerable effort to marketing his unique consultancy, integrating meditation, spirituality, righteousness, and corporate strategy. While poised for long-term benefits, he faced the challenge of corporate preferences for short-term solutions.

Shruti reminisced about significant events in recent weeks. These included her mother's return to India in August after spending six months with them, Rishi's Annaprashana Samskara, and Aryan's maiden consultancy assignments.

As the sun descended, Aryan and Shruti discovered a charming riverfront café. The family enjoyed dinner, capturing memories along the Hudson and observing the passing boats and seagulls while Rishi comfortably nestled in a high-quality stroller. They captured beautiful family photos and drove back home, planning to visit Washington to participate in the World Cultural Festival.

Blissful World Cultural Festival

As a monthly ritual since Rishi's birth, Aryan and Shruti celebrated Rishi's six months with an orphanage visit on 28 September and hosted lunch for the orphan children. Ramesh and Dr. Markesic joined them on the occasion; both had come much closer but were unsure about their wedding. They were impressed with Aryan and Shruti's unique experiences and wanted to adopt the same in their life.

Immediately after lunch, Aryan, accompanied by his small and affectionate family, drove to Washington, D.C., in his Ferrari to participate in the World Cultural Festival starting September 29th. He considered it a significant opportunity to network and market his startup. The invitation came from a close friend and "Art of Living" teacher working at NASA. The festival unfolded with vibrant live music, ranging from hip-hop to classics, world music, and the rhythmic stomps of flamenco dancers worldwide. The atmosphere stirred the soul.

Empower Limitless Vision

The mega event gathered around around 17,000 global artists representing diverse cultural traditions, offering many delectable dishes. Amidst the National Mall in DC, they joined thousands in a unified yoga flow. On the evening of September 29th, just before the majestic performances began, Rishi's laughter captured everyone's attention. **While moving toward the stage, Sri Sri Ravi Shankar paused to bless Rishi, inspiring the atmosphere.**

The World Culture Festival proved to be an unforgettable cultural spectacle, showcasing voices, talents, and creativity from across the globe. Aryan could get specific business leads from various parts of the USA and participating delegates from other countries with the help of his friends and networking efforts. Rishi's blissful smile attracted several delegates to talk with them. The symbolic power of this gathering, where people embraced their freedom to coexist and appreciate each other's uniqueness, was profound.

The festival materialized the Sangathana Sukta, the spirit of universal brotherhood, mutual love, and cooperation amongst everyone across the globe. **They felt a paradigm shift in thinking from 'TAKE' to 'GIVE,' resulting in an assured 'Happiness for Everyone.'** Trees give us Fruits. Rivers provide us with water. Nature gives us Air. We get all these for Free. Organizations mirroring the ***"Giving back to Society"*** principle, prioritizing righteous actions and humanity over hefty profit motives, sustain and grow. Word-of-mouth publicity from contented customers and society fosters loyalty and goodwill and ensures sustainability. Aryan's experience exemplifies this, as his selfless acts of the past generated unexpected support for his Startup Consultancy. He

Empower Limitless Vision

formulated a Polestar for his business, aiming **"To ignite positive transformation as a catalyst for nurturing excellence, sustaining happiness, and ensuring prosperity for all stakeholders."**

Dr. Markesic's Research Outcome

Soon after Aryan and Shruti returned from Washington, Dr. Markesic visited them and presented her Research Thesis with gratitude. She was happy and relaxed after countless nights doing her research, literature review, data analysis, and writing the research thesis. She wanted them to go through her thesis and suggest changes, if any. She was highly impressed with Aryan and Shruti's extraordinary efforts and sacrifices to inculcate spiritual values in Rishi.

Scrolling through the thesis, Aryan and Shruti admired Dr. Markesic for her honest efforts. They were keen to know how a liberal Christian doctor had portrayed their journey of following ancient Hindu rituals. They were amazed to see Dr. Markesic project them as a role model couple who researched and followed the learnings drawn from ancient wisdom to nurture their son Rishi even before conceiving him. She encouraged all prospective parents to plan for their children by following their example. **She argued that if one intends to establish a new business, build a house, or arrange finances to undertake any important initiative, then why do people fail in planning to conceive a child (boy or girl) of their choice, following ancient wisdom, and inculcate spiritual values in a child during pregnancy?** She highlighted certain areas that remained unexplored for future research:

- Though a son of their choice blessed Aryan and Shruti as they desired, the precautions and specific actions taken to conceive a baby boy must be empirically tested on a

Empower Limitless Vision

group of at least one hundred couples to draw conclusive evidence.

- Rishi was born with a golden aura radiating divinity. However, we can't scientifically identify the cause of the golden aura without adequate empirical evidence from a group of couples.
- It will take a few years to establish that Rishi has acquired the adequate spiritual qualities to be a Corporate Guru, despite the efforts put in by his parents.
- Aligning the functional vision or polestar with a deity is an excellent beginning to inculcate ethical working. However, its effectiveness and impact on employees have not yet been proven.

Interestingly, Dr. Markesic also expressed her desire to marry a like-minded person who supports her endeavor to be a member of a sample group along with her for an empirical study and to have a child of their choice.

Embarking on a New Beginning

Aryan's transformative journey comes full circle, originating from the Himalayan sage's initiation into spirituality and meditation. The journey progressed as he disseminated these profound teachings through group meditation sessions, followed by instilling human values in functional polestars.

Simultaneously, he married his soulmate Shruti, and they realized their shared dreams. They were blessed with a son radiating a golden aura who may become a Corporate Guru. Closing the loop, Aryan extended this wisdom to others by seamlessly integrating spirituality into professional and personal realms through his consultancy, Himalayan Insights.

Aryan's insights resonate with Rig Veda's timeless wisdom, showcasing the enduring relevance of Vedic philosophy in the contemporary world. His unwavering advocacy for mindfulness underscores the imperative to consider the holistic impacts of actions on organizations, society, and the environment. This book is a guiding beacon, illuminating the path toward harmonious coexistence and unparalleled success.

In an ever-changing world, where the dynamics of motivation shape individual and organizational trajectories, a Motivation Mantra becomes indispensable. Aryan's journey exemplifies the significance of perpetual adaptation and unwavering motivation amidst the evolving landscape. The forthcoming book in the Corporate Transformation Series will delve comprehensively into motivational aspects.

Taking a proactive approach towards social well-being, zero defects, and zero ecological impact is paramount for the growth and sustainability of the world for future generations. Establishing 'Self-Discipline' as a formidable business objective and becoming a role model is crucial for realizing the vision of universal well-being. This endeavor necessitates the integration of contemporary science with Vedic teachings.

Mindfulness emerges as a potent catalyst for personal and organizational growth, emphasizing the interconnectedness of choices with corporate, social, and environmental well-being. The managerial philosophy transcends profit-centric models, urging a focus on righteous actions and fostering a learning culture. It posits that success is measured in financial gains, positive transformations, and an enduring impact on individuals and society.

In a new world order, businesses must embrace a unified theory for excellence and cultivate a self-disciplined workforce that promotes human values among stakeholders while adapting to global needs. This integration demands aligning business practices with the timeless wisdom of Vedic studies.

The holistic approach outlined in the book envisions businesses not merely as profit-driven entities but as integral components of a larger ecosystem, actively contributing to the well-being of individuals and the planet.

In conclusion, "Empower Limitless Vision" is a transformative guide for those seeking a meaningful and fulfilling life. Aryan's journey is a beacon of inspiration, illustrating the profound impact of aligning with cosmic principles, fostering divinity, and awakening consciousness. The book challenges individuals and organizations to transcend conventional boundaries and aspire to a higher purpose, where success is enduring and contributes to the greater good. It beckons readers to embark on their transformative journeys, armed with the wisdom imparted within its pages, and strive to achieve everlasting success in every facet of life.

-x-

Corporate Transformation Series

The *Corporate Transformation Series* is your gateway to lasting excellence, purpose-driven success, and spiritual wisdom. These five powerful books bridge ancient Vedic knowledge with modern business challenges, offering a transformative path from personal growth to collective prosperity. The series illustrates a path to sustainable development, conscious leadership, and lasting well-being for individuals, organizations, and future generations.

Business of the Business is Ethical Business.

A Journey from Self to Infinite Leadership

Empower Limitless Vision

Book 1: Awaken Your True Self: Inspire Self, Be Visionary, Lead Transformation, Achieve Bliss

This inspiring first book follows a young engineer shattered by personal tragedy and disillusioned by corporate chaos. His search for solace leads him to the Himalayas, where a wise sage illuminates his path to enlightenment. Through rituals, meditation, and Vedic wisdom, he transcends grief, reconnects with his true essence, and learns to align with *Ṛta—the universal order*. It helps to integrate personal and professional success. It reveals how self-transformation can spark organizational growth and unlock lasting fulfillment. Start your journey where transformation begins within.

▧ Read More https://relinks.me/B0CW1MJ1NT

Book 2: Unleash Your Limitless Excellence
Discover Your Mission, Transform Self, Embrace Wisdom, Radiate Divinity, and Achieve Stupendous Success

Step into your fullest potential—personally, professionally, and spiritually. This book empowers you with practical tools to achieve multidimensional success: career growth, financial mastery, health, resilience, and inner peace. It also guides young couples in conceiving and nurturing virtuous children following Vedic rituals.

▧ Read More https://relinks.me/B0CDV439QC

Empower Limitless Vision

<u>**BOOK-3: Empower Limitless Vision:**</u> Ignite Consciousness, Inspire Divinity, Align to Cosmos, and Achieve Everlasting Success

Transcend the pursuit of excellence beyond personal goals to awaken collective purpose. Learn how organizations can craft a Shared Vision anchored in core values and Vedic deities that symbolize each business function, like Finance, HR, Quality, Marketing, and Supply Chain Management. etc. Discover how parents can nurture a child's virtues even before birth. Learn ancient ways to inculcate Samskara in a child during pregnancy.

▨ Read More https://relinks.me/B0CT4YWHJL

<u>**BOOK-4: Vedic Path to Infinite Motivation:**</u> Unleash Ancient Secrets to Overcome Stress, Learn Gayatri Meditation, Unfold Wisdom, and Achieve Blissful Success

Unlock the inner fire of motivation through the Gayatri Mantra, seamlessly blending timeless Vedic wisdom with modern success strategies. Understand the purpose of life, attain infinite motivation, align with the universe to transcend stress, ignite personal growth, and cultivate inspiring leadership. The book helps you learn to lead with calm, clarity, and compassion—a timeless guide to inspiring others and living with balance and bliss.

▨ Read More https://relinks.me/B0DMV8Y9VQ

Book 5: Infinite Leadership: Master Your Motivation, Lead Team Leaders, Inspire Greatness through Divinity, and Achieve Blissful Success

Infinite Leadership is your gateway to mastering the art of sustainable, purpose-driven leadership. Drawing from the Gayatri Mantra and Vedic wisdom, it reveals seven divine insights for inspiring greatness. At its core, it unveils the *'Vedic Blueprint of Infinite Leadership'* and *the 'Vedic Leadership Matrix'* that empower leaders to grow from within, inspire teams, and achieve blissful success for themselves, their organizations, and society. The book is a must-read for leaders seeking to elevate leadership to a **higher realm of wisdom and impact.**

▨ Read More https://relinks.me/B0F675X4V8

-x-

May I ask You for a Small Favor

At the outset, a BIG THANK YOU for taking the time to read this book. You could have chosen any other book, but you took mine, and I appreciate this.

I hope you gained at least a few actionable insights that will positively impact your daily life. <u>Would you be willing to give me 30 seconds more of your time?</u>

I'd love it if you could leave a review about the book. *Reviews are the most important input for an author. They help understand readers' needs and address them in forthcoming books. They allow the readership to grow. To put it straight, reviews are an author's breath.*

Please leave your review for this book, **Infinite Leadership**. *Please also share your feedback about the* **Corporate Transformation Series**.

It will take a minute of your time, but it will tremendously help me address your queries and expectations, reach out to more people, and impact their lives.

Please leave your FIVE-STAR review on Amazon. Click:
https://relinks.me/B0CT4YWHJL
Thanks for your support.
Be Happy! Enjoy Life! Cheer!

Balvir Talwar
btalwar1502@gmail.com